AF817104

Internet Marketing for Magazine Publishers

LINDA RUTH

Internet Marketing for **Magazine Publishers**

Cedar Crest Books
www.cedarcrestbooks.com

Cedar Crest Books
www.cedarcrestbooks.com

Internet Marketing for Magazine Publishers
by Linda Ruth

First Printing – January 2009

ISBN: 978-0-910291-05-7

Book Design by J. M. Tavenner
Photo of Linda Ruth taken by Mark Corliss

To Greg, who has moved on to working for the good
of the world, but does not forget
that he began in publishing.

ACKNOWLEDGEMENT

What I love about internet marketing is that it creates opportunities to use everything we've ever learned from advertising greats in every medium, and also to make things up as we go along. It is kind of a wild west where anything goes; yet the solutions of direct mail, TV advertising, space advertising, and even door to door are successfully applied, and the cardinal rule of direct marketing—test, test, test—remains as true to this medium as any other.

So the beginning of any set of acknowledgements would have to be to the direct marketing greats who developed the rules that internet marketers are having such fun plundering, applying, violating, and ignoring. We all know who they are—who better than they to turn their skill into an art worthy of its own hall of fame?

Today's marketers also show a talent for promoting their names along with their skills, and several of them are mentioned in this book. I admire their energy, their freshness, their enthusiasm, and their sense of playfulness as they start and fold and start companies, make and lose and make new fortunes, apply what they've learned to the internet and invent new things. They are a fun bunch, and it's well worth getting to know them and learning from their successes.

But beyond all of them, and from our own world of publishing, I want to especially thank Don Nicholas, who is much more than an internet marketer. He is a true publishing whiz, whose genius lies in identifying and codifying what works in a system and showing publishers how to apply it to their products and company. He is a teacher and a leader and a mentor; and he is very, very generous in sharing what he has learned.

Also I have to thank Elizabeth Cooper, editor and friend.

And DuCiel, who is trying these principals on her own website.

And Amy, who is our very own and quite brilliant social marketer.

And Haley, who can be counted on to give an opinion, and to weigh things.

And David Rottenberg, who told me I should go ahead and publish, and then did it for me.

CONTENTS

PART TWO

How to Bring People to Your Site

PART THREE

What to Do With Them When They Get There

INTRODUCTION

The Internet is the greatest thing that ever happened to magazine publishers. Let's start with that, and everything else will flow from it. The Internet is not a competitor (not really). It is not a death knell (not at all). The Internet is a challenge; it is a transformation; it is an epiphany. But most of all, it is an opportunity.

The Internet represents the next essential step in the transformation of magazine publishing, the transformation from words-on-paper to what it has become, what it must become: the direct communication with each individual enthusiast of each individual niche, large or small, universal or minute.

Publishers—Positioned for Profit

As publishers, we pwn. No one is better positioned than magazine publishers to enter the world of the Internet and begin to take advantage of its enormous opportunities.

There are still magazine publishers, I know, who fear the changes that the Internet represents to their print business. There are magazine publishers who see it as encroaching on their world. And there are many, many magazine publishers who believe that the Internet, for better or for worse, signals the replacement of the print world for something new; that the future is the Internet, and it is better to leap off the print train and onto the Internet jet. None of that is completely true.

What the Internet is, what it can be, is an extension of the role of the magazine publisher into a medium with greater possibilities, greater flexibility, and potentially a much, much bigger audience. It is an extension—not a replacement. Print still has an important, a currently irreplaceable role to play, although I am not going to argue this or go deeply into it here. What I will do is to show how the Internet can become a more vital, more successful part of your publishing efforts.

Consider this: the Internet is a vast field of content. People visit it for its content. And there is no greater expert in any given field of content than its magazine publisher. No one has access to more of the content, to more of the experts, to more of the celebrities in any one field. The Internet needs magazine publishers to provide it with fresh, new, constantly updated and authoritative material in every field. The archives uniquely possessed by every magazine publisher also become a great source of knowledge and information on the Web.

The Internet is also a source of entertainment. Every successful magazine publisher has long understood that diversion, recreation, entertainment must be part of the mix. Like poetry, magazine publishing must teach and delight, be informative and entertaining. These skills become part of the online mix that is the publisher's site.

The Internet is where relationships are built and maintained. What great editor's passion, what great editor's entire raison d'etre, is not about the relationship with the reader? And when it comes to building relationships online, who has a better start? Magazine publishers have the contact information; they know their readers and just how to reach them.

Magazine publishers have more that is essential to success online. Magazine publishers have writers, designers, graphic artists, layout people. They have copy editors, proofreaders, research people, and fact checkers. They have marketing people and data people, analytical people and financial people. They have all the disciplines needed for success online.

"But wait," a publisher might say. "Our online division is completely separate from our print division. We're using whole different sets of people." Whether or not the division is different, the company is the same, and the experience and expertise of magazine publishing is deeply ingrained in everything you do. This is true for your editorial, your financial, your graphics.

To some people the Internet is complicated, challenging—just plain hard. Well, magazine publishers know complicated, challenging and hard. They know what it means to coordinate a production schedule taking into account advertising closing, on sale dates, lead time, and printer schedules; to juggle multiple contracts; to manage staff from a distance; to read a distributor's remittance advice and somehow reconcile it to copies sold. They know what it means to try to get cooperation from a distributor who says your efficiency is too low, your remit too high. They know what it means to try to launch an annual publication or a one-shot when some retailers are requiring a unique bipad and others are refusing to add bipads to their system, or to face the pressure for down pricing subscriptions at the same time that postage and paper rates are climbing.

Publishers know hard, all right. And compared to what we have faced over the years, the Internet, with its potential for immediate feedback, audience connection, virtual product, flexibility, and freedom, is something we can handle. As magazine publishers, to use the jargon of the Internet, we *pwn*.

Where do Great Internet Marketers Come From?

The most successful people in Internet marketing come from, precisely, everywhere. Some were techies with a germ of an idea that they got out through an initially cult following via their own passionate interest. Some of the greatest Internet marketers came from direct sales, selling real estate, carpet cleaning, dog training and so on, on a one-on-one basis off-line, transferring knowledge and techniques online to add to the canon of Internet marketing knowledge. Others came from direct mail. The Internet, for them, became the place to use the techniques of copywriting and direct mail marketing to sell online. People from television and radio came to apply their knowledge and techniques to this new medium. The Internet is TV, they tell us from the stage at Internet conferences: The Internet is visual, it is auditory.

People come to the Internet from everywhere, and the Internet becomes an extension of who they are. Gamers, techies, movie people, publishers—their knowledge is tested, validated, adapted, applied, and absorbed into something new and different.

I came from magazine retail sales. In retail sales, the techniques of selling mentioned above are certainly important, certainly applied. But in retail sales there is also the principle of immediacy, a principle that applies, equally, to everything done online.

In magazine sales you learn the importance of content, color, impact, testing, simplicity, clarity, and obviousness. You learn the importance of telling your story at a glance. On magazine covers as in Web sites, you have a limited time to tell your story, to engage the reader. You have to let them know right away that you have the solution to the problem, the answer to the riddle, the latest news or reviews or reports.

In magazine retail sales it is a principle to not make readers work too hard, or think too much, to arrive at their conclusions. It is important to know the reader, to appeal to the reader through powerful words and key phrases that are about the reader, not about the publisher.

The lessons learned from your magazine marketing, from your magazine covers, should be applied appropriately to your Web site and your marketing along with lessons learned throughout all your disciplines. In the section that follows I'm going to show you how relevant your magazine cover is to the principles you will use on your Web site.

About This Book

In this book we will look at a small portion of the full range of opportunity, the portion having to do with marketing on the Internet. This can and should include the marketing all of your magazine business, from subscriptions of the paper product itself to the whole range of information and entertainment products you might offer.

Here you will learn the techniques of off-line selling that have been successfully transplanted to the Web, including sales letters, calls to action, persuasive sales techniques, unique-selling-proposition (USP) testimonials, and many more. You will learn the techniques of off-line selling that have transmuted into something new and different online. For example:

Direct mail: Is it the same, or not the same, through email? The answer is a little of both—and you'll find out *how* and *why*.

Knowing your customer/reader: Always the basis of magazine publishing, in fact the basis of all sales, now it can be done faster, cheaper, and more completely than ever before.

Long and short form sales letters: All the rules are not exactly the same, and you'll find out why.

Pass along readership: The opportunities that exist here will blow you away.

You will also learn new and different techniques of marketing that never existed before, that have changed the way we speak to our readers and our customers.

For example: Rather than going out to find the customer, now it is possible to make the customer come to find you.

Your readers will now bring in new readers, to a degree never envisioned before.

Your competitors are now your partners—and the partnership will make your business many times more powerful.

And this is just a beginning.

All of what I am teaching in this book can be achieved cheaply, quickly, and easily. Almost all of it has been done at one time or another by individuals, even nontechnical people, sitting alone in their homes, exploring how to implement an idea. This is completely important, because one thing holding back publishers from a full implementation of their online goals is a perceived lack of resources. But using these techniques to build your business, both online and off, is easier and faster than you would imagine.

So let's get started familiarizing ourselves with the brave new world of marketing on the Internet. We'll begin with how to build your Web site.

PART ONE

Building Your Site

Chapter One

Your Site Is Your Salesperson

To begin the discussion of Internet marketing, we have to talk about your Web site itself. Your site is your publication, it is editorial, it is social, it is entertainment. It is also your storefront, and as such it must capture visitors and convert them. Sound familiar? It's what we've always said about your cover as well.

Going back to the traditional print magazine cover, do you know what is possibly the most powerful phrase that you can put on your cover?: "how to." Now do you know what is one of the most search phrases ever on the Internet? That's right: "how to."

Should the best practices design techniques from magazine publishers be lifted straight from your magazine and applied to your Web site? Should your home page, in effect, become a magazine cover? Of course not. No more should it be a book cover, or a direct mail letter (though sometimes it should be that), or a billboard. But the principles learned are often the same and should be remembered.

For the sake of your marketing people, as you design your site, remember a few simple rules established in the world of Internet publishing and relating back to what we have always known about our magazine covers:

Keep It Simple

On a magazine cover you want to find the happiest balance between offering the most items of interest for the most people (adding more cover lines to appeal to various readers' interests) and keeping the overall look simple enough so that its impact is immediate and direct. Your Web pages have the same imperative.

For immediate, effective impact, keep your Web pages simple. Don't confuse the eye with too much activity, too many competing voices, too much clutter. Stick to just a few typefaces, fonts, type sizes, and make sure your font is legible.

Eye tracking technology shows us that the eye moves, when studying a Web page, about five times per second. While it is moving, it doesn't take in information or images; it is essentially blind. It skips from place to place, focusing on certain areas, trying to absorb what it needs quickly, and then it moves on. If your visitors can't find what they are looking for in a few seconds, or at least get a sense that they are in the right place and will find what they are looking for, they too are likely to move on. You need to immediately show your visitors that they are in the right place, that they will indeed find what they are looking for here at your site. They need to see what you are offering up front.

A cleaner site is more search-engine-friendly as well, which will help visitors find you in the first place.

Of course simplicity and legibility mean different things in print and online. In print it is widely accepted that a serif typeface, such as Times New Roman, is the easiest to read; that is the reason it is so often found as a default. Online, the serifs have been found to confuse and tire the eye. For your defaults, use Edna and Arial. For maximum legibility, minimum strain, keep your text dark on a light background.

Use Conventions Wisely

As with your sequential magazine covers, your Internet pages must include both fixed and variable elements from page to page, so that your site is easily, coherently identifiable, assuring visitors that they haven't wandered off; yet each page must be noticeably different so that they don't have to hunt to see what is unique about any given page.

While it is always up to the designer to choose which elements are the same, which will differ, it helps to know the conventions and use them. Just as, on your cover, you express your creativity, your individuality within the specific conventions that have been found to maximize sales in your field, on your Web site it makes it easier for everyone—you, your site designer, and your audience—to use specific established conventions.

Links not yet visited are underlined in blue; active links (where the mouse hovers over the unclicked link) are ordinarily found in red; visited links will be purple. Easy to find, easy to know your navigation history.

Also, when it comes to links, search engines give more value to ones that are clearly marked and easily followed from the body of the text than to ones that are buried or hidden in any way. Search engines are all about the user experience, and easy navigation is part of that.

Using conventional linking signals, you can skip using unnecessary words such as "click here." This phrase is both redundant and, when it comes to search engine ranking, useless.

Another navigational best practice is the use of "bread crumbs," those cues at the top of the page that indicate where you are in the site and how you got there. Appropriately used (small so as not to dominate; using the ">" symbol to indicate the movement from one level of the information hierarchy down to the next; bolding the "you are here" one; and not allowing it to take the place of a clear overall site navigation), these signals will aid the site visitor and clarify your Web structure.

When do you defy convention? On a testing basis, every day—just as you do with your publications. On a magazine cover, for example, we know that cover lines belong on the left, towards the top. But we always want to test. More cover lines or fewer? Right-justified for checkout? Magazine readers like to be surprised; they like to see something new, something different. On the Internet things are changing even faster. Yesterday's new idea is today's convention, and yesterday's convention is a crusty old cliché today. And testing is easy. So every day, take something from your site and test it. That includes conventions as well.

For example, we know that navigation bars must be easy to find, the navigation signals clear and easy to follow. They also have conventional placements: in a bar across the top; stacked and to the left.

Some Internet marketers have found that stacking the navigation bar on the right will raise search engine ranking and increase conversion. Why would that be? Perhaps it results in better keyword placement on the page; perhaps the site visitor sees something of more interest, earlier, than the navigation bar.

Whatever the reason, it is worth testing this—along with every other element on your site.

Location, Location, Location

I spent my entire newsstand career telling publishers to put the important items on their cover in the top left. This was to ensure that the lead cover line would be visible on a newsstand, where the front lip of the newsstand and the overlapping display made not much else visible.

Fast forward to today, when eye mapping studies have shown that top left space on your Web site to be the most important "real estate" you've got. It's where the eye goes first, stays longest. Put the most important thing you have up there.

Next the eye travels to the upper right, and then mid-left down the page. Knowing this attention flow will help you organize and prioritize your content layout on the page.

Shift for a moment now to the world of newspaper publishing: Everything important should go "above the fold." Don't make your visitors scroll. Did you know that 6 percent of them don't even know how to do it? And another good percentage of them don't want to be bothered.

That doesn't mean that you have to put everything in the first panel seen by visitors when they click onto your site. How would you do that anyway? If your site is well-designed, it has been established that visitors will stay, will scan, will scroll, will click through—*if* they are sure of finding what they want eventually. But what do you want them to see, click on, act on first? That should go top left, that should go above the fold.

Positioning and highlighting of text should complement one another. As with a good magazine cover, a newspaper or magazine page, or a well-made ad, on a Web page the elements most important to the reader, most likely to trigger some action, are the ones to highlight. There should be a clear visual hierarchy of meaning. The lead caption gets the lead line—highest, biggest, boldest. The subheads are larger and bolder than the body copy. And so on.

A last point to consider: Do not make your visitors scroll horizontally. Design your site so that the only scrolling necessary is up and down—keeping in mind that about one third of Internet users keep their browser panel open at the left of the screen, reducing the visible width of the page they have opened.

Design For Impact

As the great architect Ludwig Mies van der Rohe famously said (borrowing from a poem by Robert Browning): "Less is more." This has been found to be a valid design principle throughout the world of publishing. It holds true for your Web site design as well. Make every element count on your page. Don't have anything there which is unnecessary or detracts from the purpose.

This includes the use of images. An image can be powerful, but it also must be relevant. It should be arresting, immediate; it must tell its story at a glance.

Another bit of advice from the world of architecture: "Form follows function." In the structure of your Web site, it's a good place to start as well. Start with the function—the presenting of content, the capturing of attention, the conversion of readers—and proceed thereby to the form. But instead of function, we should perhaps really say usability, ease of use. So how about this: Form follows ease of use.

Have you ever visited a Web site where the eye is first drawn to an image that bears only a tenuous relationship to the topic of the site? As your main image on your magazine cover must relate to the lead cover line, the image on your Web site that first draws your eye must be relevant to the site theme, a lead story, or an important part of the site to which you click via the image. (For example, you might have a magazine cover icon you can click on for a story, back issue, or subscription).

Like your magazine cover, your Web site has a limited amount of time to capture and direct visitors' attention. Once again, if they see they are in the right place they will stay and browse, but if they click through to the site and are not immediately sure they are in the right place, they may just click right out of it again. Everything on that page must be quickly understandable, relevant, and compelling.

Make sure you immediately answer these questions for your visitor: "Where am I (am I in the right place)? What can I do here? How do I do it?" Don't confuse the issue; don't clutter it up with anything unnecessary.

Use size, contrast, and position to draw the eye to the places you want it to go. As on your magazine cover, don't be too "cute." Opt for clarity, opt for practicality, opt for usability. Save the cleverness, the plays on words, the obscure references and the like for the content of the articles themselves.

Not All Magazine Principles Apply

Unlike a on magazine cover, your logo does not have to be, should not be the dominant element. You need it of course, to identify your site and to identify each page. But beyond that, it should take a back seat.

You'll find that your Web site, perhaps surprisingly, is not about you. It is about your visitors: their wants, their needs, their hopes and aspirations, and how you will help them achieve them. Your logo should be visible, identifiable—and ignorable.

The Internet, after all, is more—much, much more—than one giant newsstand. But it shares with the newsstand at least one identifying characteristic. Like a newsstand, it is a battle for the visitor's attention, with the best site triumphant—that day. And as we do on the newsstand, on the Web we must treat the browser's attention as a resource that can be tapped, or it can be lost. We can't treat that attention lightly. It is finite; it can be depleted if managed poorly. But it can also be nurtured and increased. It is the source of all our success.

Chapter Two

Web 2.0: Meaningless Hype?

Before we delve further into the specifics of building your particular site, we need to stop and consider the sort of environment or context in which your site will exist, a context we call Web 2.0.

In 2004 representatives of O'Reilly Media and MediaLive International conceived the idea of Web 2.0 in a brainstorming session at a conference. It was meant to refer to the viability of the Web after the dot-com collapse in the fall of 2001, and it came to refer to a number of elements characteristic of the emerging capabilities and utilities of the Internet.

Decades prior to this, in his landmark book *Understanding Media: The Extensions of Man*, Marshall McLuhan coined the phrase "the medium is the message." He defined *medium* as "any extension of ourselves," and *message* as the changes in "scale or pace or pattern" that result from the new medium, including, or even largely consisting of, unintended consequences.

Web 2.0 is an almost complete realization of McLuhan's vision. As we progress into its domain, our ways of thinking, interacting, even being in the world are changed; and as these ways change, the Internet changes with it. Each new application or use results in newer ways of using the technology, newer ways of thinking about its possibilities. And the world opens up as the horizon continues to recede.

Web 2.0 is the knower, the known, and the process of knowing, all contained in one place. As we use this technology, we continually create it, and it us. The point of Web 2.0 is that the ways we think about and use the Web have evolved dramatically over the years. What we can do online is dynamic and synergistic and alive.

A print product is one part of that, an important part. But publishers who are still asking themselves the question: "Should I post my content on the Web?" have yet to catch up with the amazing potentiality that exists for them.

Web 2.0 is essentially the Web as living, breathing, evolving thing. Its characteristics, too, are emerging. They include *participation*, *customization*, *evolving systems*, *easy access*, "*long tail*" *outreach*, and, to an unprecedented extent, *sharing*.

Participation

Your readers are no longer just your readers. They are your co-creators. Think conversation, user-generated content, content-sharing sites, social-media sites, finding friends, making friends, networking. This is what people come to the Web to do. It is what your site must offer if it is to be relevant, viable, and long-lived.

Without these elements your site is perceived as an inert thing, once viewed not returned to. Even continuous updating of content alone won't be sufficient to draw the denizens of Web 2.0. Think social networking: MySpace, Facebook, LinkedIn, Twitter. Think content sharing: Ezine.com, Squidoo, HubPages, YouTube, Flickr. Think social bookmarking: Del.icio.us, Digg, StumbleUpon. These sites are all reflective of the participatory, user-generated, ever-evolving lifestyle that people look for on the Web.

And who better to shape this emerging world than magazine publishers, whose entire reason to be has been based upon the reader, who have nurtured a dialog with the reader and responded to the reader's wishes? Magazine publishers have long known that opportunities for reader participation and responsiveness to reader feedback are what generate loyal readers. Now the Internet offers a previously unheard of level of immediacy, effortlessness, and speed to the process.

Customization

What users find when they visit the Web very much depends on what they are looking for and, more importantly, who they are. It is reflected in their choice of networks, news, product reviews, links, and bookmarks. Never has there been such an opportunity to know the audience, down to each individual person. Never has there been the opportunity to respond so quickly.

Evolving Systems

As users participate in the dynamic unfolding of this Web 2.0 world, systems grow, change, and are tweaked to meet the new needs. New things are created, old ones fall by the wayside. Because what emerges is based on user needs, wants, and behavior, there is no real roadmap for this growth. It is not predetermined, not predictable. To paraphrase the poet Theodore Roethke, we learn by going where we have to go.

These systems are organized by how people think, rather than by some theory or template of functionality. They adapt based on how participants behave, in order to enrich user experience. One day there is a new social media site, the next it is linked to Facebook and YouTube, and the next you pick up a line of code from the one site to embed in any site. One day you browse for an interesting blog, the next you set up an RSS feed so the top blogs will come to you. One day you hire a programmer to add this cool new application to your Web site, the next you pick it up as freeware.

This applies to content as well. One day you have books and special reports available for sale online; the next, those very books and special reports are available for free to loyal site participants, and new releases are available.

Easy Access

This feature of Web 2.0 has been tested by magazine and newspaper publishers in their search for monetization and found valid. Alternatively, if you set up a barrier between site visitors and content, more frequently than not the visitor will not convert to a participant. At the leading edge of Web marketing, many sites now give away valuable content without even requesting or requiring an email address. Sites that have made the barriers for entry higher are finding that this strategy is incompatible with the easy-access nature of Web 2.0.

Long Tail Outreach

Not long ago, Chris Anderson, who coined the phrase and introduced it in *Wired* magazine, commented that magazine publishers had not yet found a way to capitalize on the "long tail" of Web 2.0.

Long tail is a principle we'll expand on in future chapters, along with keyword searches, segmentation, and targeting. What long tail is, very simply, is a more targeted way of reaching people. It subverts the old 80/20 principle (20 percent of your efforts result in 80 percent of your profit) and allows for greater accessibility of less-frequent searches.

While it's understandable that magazines (whose very existence in the consumer market initially depended on an appeal to a mass audience) still operate with a "short tail" philosophy, nevertheless there is an enormous opportunity here.

Special-interest print publications have found that increasing specialization has diminishing returns. For example, although a "cat" publication might have more chance of success than a "pet" publication (because a certain degree of targeting is a plus, as a rule), a "Persian cat" publication might begin to lose some market; and a magazines for certain specialized owners of Persian cats—say, those who live in California, or those who go to cat shows, or those whose cats are a certain color—will lose more readers still (though possibly providing a more attractive buy to very qualified advertisers).

On the Internet, however, it is possible to have it both ways. You can have a publication and a Web site for cat owners, with subsets of forums, blogs, information feeds, products, and advertising for increasingly narrow niches of cat owner interests.

Sharing

Openness, radical decentralization, and trusting strangers: Open-source software shows how far these concepts can be taken. You can go to a Web site and pick up a template for a social media site—completely preprogrammed, turnkey, ready to go—for free. You can go to a Web site and pick up your blogging software and drop it into your own site, again for free. You can find software that you can use today, tomorrow, every day that is continually evolving, continually improving, continually updated, by users from all over the world.

Small bits of new code are constantly appearing and being shared via email, instant message, blogs and Web sites. A widget is sent and uploaded, and now thousands of people can automatically stream the latest celebrity interview, see the weather forecast in their home town, on their home page. Facebook members create applications that are added to the site and soon shared by thousands of people.

And it isn't only software of course; far from it. It is content too. Social media sites allow participants to create their own mini-sites, uploading their widgets, their videos, their audios, and their blogs. Wikis allow experts and novices to add to the information base, demonstrating the Web 2.0 concept of radical trust.

In this world, of course, the concept of ownership also changes. Web 2.0's architecture is that of participation; it exists through services, rather than a stagnant and prepackaged software. It is non-localized. And, back to the concept of easy access, for the most part it's free.

What Google Thinks is Important is Important

The Internet changed our ways of communicating, participating, interacting. Web 2.0 has changed it yet again. A very short time ago, the big retail news was that Wal-Mart had become the largest seller of music in the world. Today they have been surpassed by iTunes. Tomorrow it may be something else again. Web 2.0 is part of that.

As Conversation Domination founder Howie Schwartz likes to say, "This is not your mother's Google." If you pay attention just to Google, he tells us, you can run your entire business based on what you learn. What Google thinks is important is what is important, and what *will* be important, in the evolving online world; and what Google cares about today is all based on Web 2.0.

When Google bought YouTube for the oft-cited sum of $1.6 billion, they showed that user-generated content was of importance. That's something to watch. They went on to buy Jaiku, the microblogging site, and other Web 2.0 properties—something to watch.

Wouldn't you think that paying attention to what the search engines buy is going to shed some light on what will be emphasized in search? And of course, an understanding of how search works is a basis of all Internet success.

When Google launched Google 2.0 they were showing that the emphasis on well-established sites, the cyber-equivalent of a brick and mortar business, sites that have longevity and a history, was changing. The new Google began to include images, books, videos, directory listings in first page search results. For established Web sites, this meant pushing listings farther down the page—perhaps off page one of search results entirely.

Google began to emphasize recency of posting as a search element. A blog or a Twitter update or a new Squidoo lens could push an established Web listing down even further, this despite years of conscientious SEO (search engine optimization) work.

What this tells us, one of the things it tells us, is that Google sees Web 2.0 as important, significant, relevant—and is betting their company on it. And yes, what Google thinks is important, we need to see as important too.

So Web 2.0? Not a fad. Not a lot of meaningless hype. And definitely, absolutely not irrelevant to your Web site, or anyone else's.

Chapter Three

What are you selling?

The question that seems to bedevil many magazine publishers when it comes to putting up a site on the Internet is what, exactly, are they selling? Is the Web site a subscription sales site? Is it a free-content site whose purpose is branding? Are they in transition to all-digital to save costs and keep up with the times? Will they build their sites and sell space to advertisers? Will theirs be a membership site that you have to pay to enter? What are the products, and how can publishers monetize all this information that it is their vocation and avocation to assemble?

Of the models above, there are breathtaking successes that you could point to where magazine publishers have made it work, and breathtaking (and forgotten) failures where it didn't. There are also case histories of what works best and why it works.

Some fundamental principles have been proven:

Web Site Content is Free

If you are looking for browsers that are searching the history of guitar picks, for example, or how to tie a knot or how to catch a fish, know that your prospects will find on the Web the information they seek, whatever that information may be. If someone navigates to your site and has to pay to join, even if the price is as low as a sign-up with full contact information, the visitor is likely to go elsewhere.

So while there is a certain level of success to be had in membership Web sites, experience shows that people are unlikely to commit to them when they have other options—and they do, they always do have other options.

Newsletters Are Free

Not only should the greater part of the content on your Web site be free, but your regular e-newsletters should be as well. It is too late to roll back the clock; the standard has been set, and what has been found, once and again, is that people will not pay for an email newsletter, regardless of the quality of the content. They are used to getting it free, and that is not going to change widely any time soon.

What You Can Get With Your Content Are Names

By virtue of your content, you prove yourself an expert, someone to be trusted, and—ideally—a friend. You use your content to begin to build a relationship with each visitor to your site; you use your content to convert the visitor to a site participant. If people have sampled your content and found it good, they are usually willing to exchange their email addresses for the promise of additional content. This is the beginning of your marketing effort.

Products Can Be Sold

What are the products that you can sell? Special reports, e-books, audio courses, video courses, software. People are used to finding free content on the Internet. They are also used to paying for courses. Your wealth of knowledge and information can easily be packaged into formats that have monetary value to your audience and then sold to them based on the strengths of the relationships you are building.

Subscriptions Can Be Sold

Publishers have had mixed results posting their complete publication every issue online. Some have found that it actually increased the subscriptions of their print publication; to others it looked as if they decreased as a result. To me, this is a moot point. If a publisher is still asking can they put their publication up online, they are asking the wrong question. If they are looking to post their magazine content, they are still very, very far from appreciating the power and flexibility and utility of this medium. They are in print-think, not in Web-think.

Get away from thinking about posting your print publication, and think about what you can put online that can't be in your publication. How about video snippets of the destination described in today's issue of a travel magazine? How about digital resources for snazzing up reader scrapbooks for a scrapbooking magazine? You could go on and on.

But whatever you are doing with your content, you shouldn't lose sight of selling your print publication on your site. Allow your circulation people prime space on every page to make their case and convert.

Ad Space Can Be Sold

Ads are of course a valid and effective way to monetize your site, and many Internet publishers have created lucrative businesses simply driving traffic in large numbers to a site and then selling ads through Google Adsense, supplemented with their own advertising space sales.

Much can be said about selling advertising space on your Web pages; however, an in-depth discussion of the topic is outside the scope of this book. Certainly, though, it is another way of creating revenues and profits for your site.

From here we go on to the core message of this book: how to reach your customers and sell your products on the Internet.

PART TWO

How to Bring People to Your Site

Chapter Four

Search Engine Optimization: A Moving Target

From a magazine publisher's point of view, search is essentially newsstand. In both cases you are engaging the people we call browsers: potential buyers scanning for something that holds interest. On the Internet, if you are present with your search term, you have a chance of getting to that next step: the click-through, the purchase. In both cases—on the newsstand with your cover, on the Web with your search term—just being there has consumer value, adds to your visibility, adds to the recognition of your product and of your Web site.

In both cases you can split test to gauge differences in the customer's response to what you are offering. In both cases, you are not marketing by interrupting what they are doing. You are catching your customers while they are looking for something that you might offer.

Organic search, or natural search is what brings most people to your site. Search engine optimization (SEO) comprises all the things we do to optimize the process of natural search without advertising.

Maybe you remember the early days, when we were all setting up our first Web sites and SEO was all about density, and algorithms, and submitting your site to the of *thousands* of search engines out there on a regular basis and getting a zillion random links into your site, and no one really knew for sure what it all was about? SEO has changed a lot since then, and today it's easier, a *lot* easier. This is not to say there aren't still lots of aspects to it; and no matter what you do, there is still always more to do. It's a moving target, and the process is never really complete.

What I'm going to outline here are some basic principles to give you a start. These principles are actually some of the most important things you can know and do in SEO. The thing to remember, always, is that a search engine exists to make the user experience as easy and successful as possible.

It's an ongoing process of improving the system to get the best possible search results for any possible search term entered. The whole system tends to go in the direction of greater simplicity and ease of use.

Getting to Page One

The purpose of SEO is to make your Web site maximally visible by delivering the most frequent and best-ranked listings in search results. The higher your site is in search rankings, the more people are likely to click through.

Search engines use Web crawlers or spiders to visit all available Web sites, create copies, index them, and rank them according to search algorithms. The algorithms are constantly changing to meet the needs of people doing the searches more quickly and to deliver the best results. SEO looks at a Web site's coding, structure, links, click-throughs, and other factors to improve a site's search engine ranking, or where it appears in a list of "hits" in response to a given typed-in search.

Approaches to SEO are multiple. Today they must include all aspects of Web 2.0. They also require a familiarity with Google 2.0. Google, while not the only search engine, is well over half the search market. And where Google leads, others tend to follow.

Google 2.0 is universal search, pulling from everywhere. This means that Google searches now draw results from separate properties covering books, local directory information, images, news, and video. Google 2.0 came about because people were leaving Google and going elsewhere for their searches—to YouTube, for example, before YouTube became a part of Google. Google 2.0 is Google's way of providing a better search experience.

Changes like this mean that your traditional SEO techniques won't always win. The traditionally defined "strength" of your domain will no longer guarantee, or even necessarily deliver, search rankings. The recency of a posting is replacing the authority of a site. In short, Google has changed the rules, *again*. And Google will continue to change the rules. Search, and its optimization, will continue to evolve.

This is an enormous opportunity, of course. By watching what climbs to page one—blog postings, video, social media and content sharing sites—publishers have an "in" to the process, a way of leapfrogging the traditional process and landing on page one.

It's Web 2.0 again. Dynamic, relevant, and necessary. And while not replacing the other, more traditional optimization techniques described here, it takes its place alongside them.

Put on Your White Hat

Beyond Google, essentially all search engines are constantly evolving. To keep people from spamming the system, and to continue to make searches very successful for people, the search engines continue to refine their algorithms. Sometimes that results in tweaks that we need to make in our search optimization. What yesterday we could define and defend as optimizing our keyword density, today might be seen as keyword spam, and we could be penalized as a result. What had been yesterday's linking strategy, today might be link spam.

It is the search engines, not the sites, that define spam. It is the search engines that set up and publish the guidelines. Google, for example, articulates its list of best practices in its "Webmaster Guidelines." With that in mind, a rule that should be very comfortable for publishers to follow is this: *Optimize your site for the search engines, but create it for your audience.*

On the Web, as in print, there will be publishers who churn out junk to capture advertising dollars. They churn out useless content, even machine-generated content, even gibberish. They post sneaky redirects, wherein you click on a search term and are delivered to an irrelevant page. They load a page with hidden keywords. Through search algorithms or through the manual policing that the search engines do, the perpetrators are discovered, and they lose their search rankings.

Work with the search engines, and you will be rewarded. Try to trick them (in the world of the Internet that's called "black hat" techniques or, more simply and directly, "spamming") and you will be penalized. Be careful that your SEO provider is working completely within the so-called "white hat" code. Black hat techniques might bring a short term boost to search rankings, but in the long run they do more harm than good.

Chapter Five

Know Your Own Keywords

When I work with magazine publishers on optimizing their covers for their newsstand and subscriber interest, I have one piece of advice that is often new to them, advice that, when implemented, can make a significant difference in the consumer response to their products. It is this:

Survey your customers: Find out what key words or phrases are most important to them, and get those key words or phrases on the cover of your magazine, issue after issue.

Say that you publish a cooking magazine and, through surveying your customers and offering them word choices, you find that your number one keyword is "pasta." Without taking over the cover image or even the lead cover story, there are a thousand ways make sure there is some pasta content in each issue and to get that or something similar on every cover: "100 ways to cook pasta"; "Use pasta for make-ahead meals"; 'Plan a romantic pasta dinner"; "Low budget pasta meals."

This kind of optimization is an essential part in aiding newsstand browsers to find and select a magazine to meet their needs.

Not surprisingly keywords are an integral part of search optimization as well. And the sheer glorious ease of finding keywords that appeal to your audience, and ascertaining the degree to which they appeal, is something that we could only dream of before the Internet.

Keywords are selected to drive traffic to your site. It's that simple. What is your audience looking for? What words are they including in their searches? Find those words and build them into your site.

This is not a random or scattershot approach. It has nothing to do with guesswork. It is something you can do quickly, easily, and for free. The first step is to create an overall keyword strategy.

Developing Your Strategy

A well-thought-out keyword strategy goes way beyond just identifying the major keywords on your site, or even the main keywords in your category. A comprehensive keyword strategy is your way of identifying your customers—both the more generally interested ones and the very most targeted ones. How does this work?

The keywords come from your content and as such are very appropriate; however, it is also important to identify the specific keywords for which people are most often searching.

To take an easy example, if your magazine is about women's fitness, and you want to maximize the Internet part of your site, you would begin by taking "women's fitness" as a keyword phrase. Or would you? Are people searching for your kind of content under "women's fitness," or "women's health," or "exercise," or perhaps something else altogether—"beauty," "weight loss," "feeling better?"

Begin your strategy by brainstorming all the appropriate keywords to your site—or all the keywords you believe are appropriate. Then go online to a Web site such as Wordtracker [www.wordtracker.com]—there are plenty of free and low cost tools out there you can use—and have the site do a keyword search. It will list your keyword with relevant keyword phrases (for example, for "exercise," it might give "exercise for weight loss," "Pilates exercise," "outdoor exercise," and so on).

Google Adwords also has a keyword tool, one that suggests related keywords for the keywords you've suggested. You can grab those keywords and run them again through your keyword tracking tool.

Also, a search for a specific term on Google may turn up a bar showing related searches. In essence, Google is telling you what people who are searching your term are also searching. Simply paying attention to these related searches can provide important keywords or phrases for you.

At one time it was important to optimize for plural versus singular and even for misspellings, but search engines have begun to take these factors into account in their algorithms. Do optimize for alternate versions of a word: for example, "building" in addition to the root word "build."

A more targeted keyword is very likely to be more effective than a less targeted one. If your publication and site are about building log homes, the keyword "homes" will be hard to rank high for, and the visitors it brings to the site very well might not be interested in your specific niche. "How to build a log home," "log home building" and even "luxury log home" or "small home" or "cabin" might bring the most targeted visitors to your site.

As you compile your list of keywords and begin to use them on your site, you'll discover some keywords bring people to your site who look it over but don't sign up for anything, and maybe don't return. Other keywords might bring people that sign up for your lists, stay on your lists, and never, ever buy anything. And still others will bring you visitors that stay longer, convert better, buy more—essentially becoming full participants in your online presence. Over time, you'll even find that certain keywords deliver visitors that stay with you as participants, subscribers, or customers for a longer period of time—in essence, audience members that renew better.

For that reason, and because user information and browser preference is constantly changing, keyword research is an ongoing effort, never finally finished. And with this in mind, you can see that keyword research offers a wonderful, simple insight into the minds of people who visit the Web, and who visit your site. It essentially becomes one soldier in your research army, one way to bring in valuable information about audience needs, desires, wants, and aspirations.

Here Google Adwords also has an interesting possible function. You can begin running pay-per-click tests, in which you test specific adwords for response. This shortens the time it would ordinarily take you to test keywords on an organic basis and allows you to start compiling keyword results immediately.

Over time you will continue to add to and refine your keyword list, to find new and more effective keyword clusters, and to refine your use of keywords throughout your site. As you do so, you will begin to work with the individual pages of your site to optimize them for specific keywords and key phrases.

Using Keywords in Site Content

In simplest terms, your more general keywords will lead a visitor to your home page; the more specific or targeted keywords will lead a visitor to other pages in the site. For example "log home" might lead to your home page, "how to insulate a log home" might lead to a second-tier content page, and "log home grout" might lead to a resource page or a catalog page.

Your keywords should be included in the page names, headlines, and captions of the page. They should be at the beginning of the phrase. For example a phrase such as "log homes: best building techniques" is better than "10 things to remember when building your log home."

Use keywords in some of your page links. You'll find that if you have planned and constructed your site coherently, the page content itself should more or less take care of this. After all, your keywords are likely to be what the page is about, and that content will be found throughout the page. However, I have seen many, many sites with the keywords omitted from the headlines, weaker versions of keywords used for headlines, and keywords placed at the end, rather than the beginning of headlines.

Use Your Keywords But Don't Abuse Them

Too much repetition of keywords in your site content is considered keyword spam and you will lose search ranking because of it. Don't use your keywords more than a couple of times in the first three paragraphs, and then every few paragraphs after that.

In fact, even aside from keywords, it is important to review your Web pages to make sure each contains primarily unduplicated content. Too much of the same content, repeated from page to page in your site, will cause you to lose ranking. If you have a site with lots of pictures and the caption text is almost identical from page to page (this could be the case in some kinds of specialty shopping pages, for example), then you need to add text or change descriptions. Your shopping cart pages need content too.

If you have much of the site description duplicated over from page to page with little new text you will lose ranking. And do NOT copy text over from page to page and just throw in a handful of new keywords, a few new captions, or a smattering of new text. Write something original for every page of your site, for every cluster of keywords you are working to optimize. Make sure that each page has fresh unduplicated content for best results.

Optimize for Long Tail Searches

Use modifiers, as many as you can think of or have revealed as important through your keyword research, in writing your content. For example, on your log home Web site, maybe people are searching "cozy log home," or "antique log home" or "classic log home." Maybe they're searching "cozy mountaintop scenic modern log home." This, by the way, is the so-called "long tail" search. Obviously you'll get fewer people making that search than the more general search. But why not take up Chris Anderson's Web 2.0 challenge and optimize for the long tail searches as well as the short? Remember that the modifiers don't negatively affect the fact that your key search term, log home, is in the phrase.

Long tail, however, is not about the number of words in a search query. It has more to do with the intent of the people searching—where they are in a sales funnel, how conversion-ready they are. A general, broadly focused keyword will draw in more browsers, fewer buyers. A tightly focused, long tail keyword might draw in fewer browsers, but those they bring in will be more ready to take the conversion steps that you have set up for them to take.

Site Pages and Internal Links

As you go deeper into your site, from greater generality to greater specificity, your pages will begin to bring more targeted customers, with more specific search needs.

An internal page on your site will give page rank to your home page or other site pages it is connected to based on inbound links. In other words, the more that links into the page, the higher the search value it can give to other pages; similarly, the more links to other site pages the page in question has, the more each individual link is reduced in link value—the overall link value of the page being divided among the other pages it links to.

Links marked clearly (blue, underlined) for easy navigation are respected more by search engines than those not marked or hidden in tiny print on the page.

For every internal link that does not have search value, create a "nofollow." This little bit of coding will show search engines not to follow that link. So for your home page, you can do a nofollow for your contact page and other housekeeping pages that don't have to show up in search engines.

For your internal pages, add nofollow to links to the site map. The site map is important for SEO, but from the perspective of the search engines it is only needed on the home page.

Your resource page also need only be a "follow" link from the home page; from all internal pages it can be nofollow.

A word about the site map: it helps search engines find and index the content of your site, and as such should always be included, though it will rarely be used by visitors. It can, however, be optimized with some text and descriptions and even a call to action for visitors who find their way to it.

The Coding Aspect

Some SEO experts whom I've spoken to say that the HTML tags are no longer relevant, as search engines are now looking at the page content itself and not so much at the tags. Tags, they say, can be spammed—that is, filled with content not relevant to the page itself to force higher page rankings and bring in unwary traffic. So increasingly, search engines are not bothering with what you put in tags and instead are creating the ranking based primarily on page content.

As of now, however, most SEO experts are still recommending tag optimization. As long as there is still some relevance to those tags you might as well optimize them. After all, why not?

In briefest terms: make sure your keywords are found in your headlines, subheads, and summaries, as well as your meta title, meta description, meta keyword, and URL (Uniform Resource Locator) tags.

Make sure each of your site pages has a title of five to ten words comprising a couple of your primary keyword phrases. This is the phrase that shows up on the search and is clicked by the searcher. Word it like an ad headline, and have your search term included.

Include search terms and keywords in the keyword meta tag and the description meta tag for each page.

By the way, you will want to validate your code, which essentially means just checking for errors. You can go to W3C Markup Validation Service [http://validator.w3.org]. It isn't hard, and in my experience the corrections are usually pretty simple.

Chapter Six

Link Building and Other SEO Strategies

The whole concept of linking and link building has changed a lot over the last decade or so. Links are still an important part of your SEO strategy—really a fundamental part. But today you are not looking for sheer massive numbers of links. As I've mentioned, the search engines are onto the fact that many of the links established are completely irrelevant, they're onto the fact that people are trying to set up vast networks of interlinked sites, and they are not buying it. They see that kind of behavior as link spam, and it is being penalized.

Actually there is a lot of black hat stuff going on in the link world. There's content spam, wherein people post useless content in forums, on blogs, or in content sharing sites in order to get their links posted (many sites have created "nofollow" tags for the Web addresses posted as a result). There's "link farming," wherein entire content sites are set up for the whole purpose of linking to a main site (harder to detect, and not always even black hat, but findable and punishable if the network is completely interrelated and consistent in its linking strategy). Remember, links to sites that have no value to your site visitors can actively hurt your page rank. So your link strategy has to be sound.

Factoring in Page Rank

To figure out the potential value of a link, you can look at the page rank that the linking site has. The higher the page rank, the more valuable the link to you. So on a scale of one to ten, ten is the best, zero the worst.

You can check the page rank of all your competitors that place above you in a Google search and find out what page rank you need in order to rank above them. So for example, if those competitors showing up on page one of the results of a particular Google search happen to rank four or five, then you only need to improve your ranking to six in order to rank above them.

You do this by developing more incoming links from higher quality pages, pages that have higher rankings themselves.

There are sites that sell links to SEO people, and this does detract from the value of these links, even taking into account a high page rank.

Link swaps used to be considered an important part of a link-building strategy. They don't have as much effect any more. Search engines discount reciprocal links, and the outgoing links on your site bring down your own value.

For this reason, and because of the possibility of immediate results based on Google 2.0—posting video, blogging, and so on—there are people who will tell you that a link strategy is no longer relevant. But this is just not the case.

Linking is still relevant, still fundamental, still indispensable to your strategy. And the absolute top-of-the-line gold standard link to get is a one-way link from a highly ranked page linking to you because of the editorial value of your site. So your strategy should be simply to have the editorial that has great enough value to make other sites want to link to you.

Basically, the same great value that brings people to your site is what earns the link recognition that will drive your page rankings higher. There's a trend in Internet marketing today to chide Web site owners for looking for "traffic." You are not looking for traffic, Web marketers say; you are looking for people.

This is a clarification that magazine publishers just don't need. No group is more aware of the audience as more than just a credit card to buy products (if you can talk them into it). Magazine publishing was built around the relationship between editorial and audience, between content and people. Broadening our media platform is not likely to make us forget that.

You can compare your site's page rank with those of your competitors pretty easily by using tools available online. Google Toolbar's got a page rank analyzer that you can use on your site and theirs. If, using such a tool, you find a competitor's page rank is much higher than yours, there are also plenty of online tools you can use to find out who is linking to your competitor's site. Those would be high-priority links to go after.

The best way of proposing linking, and the way that delivers the highest-quality links, is to go to the most relevant Web sites and propose an editorial link. For example, in building link affiliations for a parenting newsletter, we found that many very relevant sites were willing to add a link to a resource list. More valuable—to both sites—was when we added some free content to the site with a link back to ours. Alternatively, where our site could legitimately provide content missing from theirs, our partner sites were willing to add a "for more information" link in or under specific articles themselves.

Directories Are Still Relevant

Directory submission is another SEO approach that has lost prestige in recent years; however I've been working with Internet sites that have gained ranking and traffic through extensive directory work. There are many paid and free directories you can submit your site to and get a listing. The main two are Yahoo and DMOZ. Yahoo does cost, but it also will give a boost to your ranking. DMOZ is a volunteer-run free directory. There may also be a directory specifically for your area of interest; you can find it with a simple Web search.

P.R. is a Search Tool

P.R. is not only a basic marketing tactic; it's also search tool. In part perhaps because it's easy and cheap, some Internet marketers discount it. Other Internet marketers swear by it, however, and point to it as a factor in many of their successes.

Submit your press releases to PRWeb [www.prweb.com]. PRWeb has both a paid and a free service. Your releases will be searched: Press releases, once indexed, tend to have search value that lasts well beyond the life of any print release you could have done.

Your press release will be picked up by Google News and other news services; it will also, and primarily, be picked up by numerous sploggers who attempt to create advertising value using other people's content harvested from the Internet for their own fake blogs. Sploggers typically pick up only the first 40 words of content, so make sure your anchor text appears within those 40 words and you may get some value from this after all.

Chapter Seven

SEO and Web 2.0

There are a number of simple ways you can leverage Web 2.0 to enhance your search rankings.

Make the Most of Your Blog (and Everyone Else's)

While it is not a substitute for the continuously updated content of your Web site, is a great way to add fresh content every day. Your blog will only require a few minutes a day to update, and if it is fresh, interesting, revealing, controversial, your audience will want to read it.

The great thing, of course, is that you can submit it to the various RSS feeds—one example is RssReader—so that people scanning blog news and updates will have it included. Another great thing is that people can download the RSS feed, include it as part of their sites, reference it in their own blogs, and so on.

Blog content can be text, of course, but ideally it should include graphics, audio, and video; it should be in a format wherein it can be downloaded onto MP3 players and played later as a podcast.

You can take all the content you create—webinars, teleseminars, training programs—and excerpt it for your blog, repurposing it in all the above ways and including links to source material or landing pages offering paid or free access to the source material.

iTunes will post your podcast content for free. This is no small deal given the market dominance of iTunes. Other services, such as Traffic Geyser, will build your podcast from audio content.

While you're blogging yourself, go out and post comments on other people's relevant blogs as well. You are probably familiar with most of the visible blogs in your subject area, and you can easily find others using software tools such as Comment Kahuna (see the Resources section at the end of this book). Comment Kahuna will search for blogs in your key subject area and show you if the blog allows links that can be clicked through; it also shows the ranking of the blog. Posting to other people's blogs gets you visible, enhances your reputation, and establishes backlinks to your site.

Pinging is, briefly, the process of letting search engines know that a new blog entry has been posted. If you enter the URL of your blog into Ping-O-Matic [http://pingomatic.com] and set it to ping, it will do so automatically to Yahoo, Technorati, and some other key sites; Google Blog Search has a pinging service [http://blogsearch.google.com]; Pinggoat will ping some smaller feed readers.

Feedburner is a good tool for tracking who is reading your blog, incorporating tagging, and actually has a lot of other applications that as a blogger you'll find handy, maybe indispensable.

Posting lists of blogs that recently linked to you will encourage bloggers in the activities that help provide these links.

Forums and SEO

The user-generated content on your sites is great for search rankings. First of all, forums in and of themselves will bring people to your site: They're going to come to join the community, to ask their questions and share their expertise in the topics you cover. In addition, the contributions of the forum participants actually increase, perhaps substantially, the searchable content on your site. This content will bring links into your site; and you can create anchor text to other pages in your site as well. And in basic SEO terms, these contributions of your site participants are going to be packed with the keywords relevant to your audience. After all, they are going to write about what they are interested in!

In fact, the forum postings and responses to your blogs can give you great ideas for articles in your print publication, future directions for your site, even additional products to offer. It's all right there, the greatest needs, aspirations, fears, pains, desires, and wants of your audience in the forum postings and blog responses.

Of course you'll want to read the forum postings yourself—who wouldn't?—to get such an inside view into the mind of your readers, so fresh, and updated daily. But there are also tools available to allow you to essentially scan the daily content and immediately see the major issues—and major keywords—posted for that day. Go to www.tagcrowd.com and you will find such a tool. Use it to scan the daily postings and it will create a "tag cloud" showing visually the phrases most repeated. There are some keyword, content, and product ideas for you in a nutshell.

Chapter Eight

Social Media

Another way to build your audience, in addition to simply drawing people into your site, is to go out and find them. More and more businesses are leveraging the power of social media such as Facebook, MySpace, and a host of other such sites and services. As David Kirkpatrick of *Fortune* tells it: "If there's a consensus in technology, it's that the next big thing after Google [...] is social networking." [September 19, 2007]

Just as at one time email represented the Internet for many, today many people equate the Internet with social networking—it is the Internet experience as far as they are concerned.

So as a marketer in search of an audience, if you want to go out and find people on the Internet, go to where they hang out. And the place they are hanging out in droves are the social media sites.

Social Networking and Social Marketing

Social marketing is a convergence of advertising, PR, and SEO. It's a fundamental pillar of "Search 2.0" (SEO in a Web 2.0 world), one of the power tools that leverage the power of the search engines to bring up listings once unavailable.

Social marketing has been lionized, vilified, identified as the current great thing, identified as the latest empty fad. Don't get sucked into any of that. Social marketing exists; it's there, and it's a tool. You don't put all your eggs in that basket, neither do you ignore it. Properly understood, properly used, it can give you a lot of benefit.

Start by setting up an account on the main social media sites—MySpace, Facebook, and any specific to your area of interest or drawing lots of people in your audience. Visit some groups, make some friends.

You can go to Ning [www.ning.com] and set up your own social media site for your own category. While you're doing that, you can go to Magazine Dojo [www.magazinedojo.com] and join the magazine publishers already using that site.

On these sites, sign up for groups that are relevant to your topic. If yours is a crafting magazine, join a few craft groups. For the log home magazine, join some log home groups.

It makes sense to do this anyway, because it keeps you close to the people who make up your market, what they are saying, what they are thinking, and who they're talking about. Are there new names in your market, new trends, new ways of thinking? You'll hear about them there.

Then start to answer questions; give out good information. Don't make a sales pitch (please). Instead, just build trust with the group, establish yourself as an authority.

This has a couple of benefits. The people reading your comments in the forums and groups, who are growing in respect for your site and its expertise, will begin to come to your site. Depending on the readership of the specific forums, the specific posts, it could be a lot of people.

Also, having your name and site address in the posts—sometimes you could point people to your site to answer a specific question or solve a specific problem (but not to sell anything, that's considered rude), other times you just have your URL as part of your signature—will raise your search rankings.

You might also start a group of your own. Set up a business page, or several pages, on Facebook; get your audience members to come as fans. Give them a reason to visit—put up a short video, offer a relevant widget, or give bits of news, tell a few jokes. From there you point people to your Web site, either the home page or other, deeper pages as appropriate to the topic at hand.

You can use a Facebook page to offer tips to your audience, to post your covers, to review a product, or to share some news. You can include a feed from your blog and other relevant blogs.

Does this sound rather basic and ho-hum? Does it sound scattershot? It doesn't matter. This kind of starter social-media work may not be the kingpin of your audience-building campaign, but it has an effect. Why walk away from anything that has an effect? Why turn away from the sites that draw the most traffic on the Internet?

I was working with someone who had a real estate magazine in Florida. By using this, along with a handful of other social media strategies I'll mention here, she went from page eight in search listings to page one in two days.

Paul Colligan of Submit To iTunes, whose specialty is podcasting, tells a story of how he wanted to accomplish two goals: to introduce a new term into the market and to see how quickly that term would be indexed. He chose a term of his own creation: Ubersyndication. He posted a question on a few microblogging sites: "Has anyone heard of Ubersyndication?"

Within minutes a couple of microbloggers had picked up the term. And after only a few minutes more, a Google search turned up several listings. Two weeks later a Google search turned up over 500 entries on the term.

I've spoken to one or two publishers who have concerns about sprinkling their content throughout the Internet, rather than having it all consolidated on a master site and other sub sites that will feed it. This is definitely the thinking of old media. This is not meant as a put-down—I am a magazine person, and am filled respect for the storehouse of knowledge and experience we have developed in so-called "old media." This young know-it-all whippersnapper of a "new media" doesn't have all the answers—look at all the booms and busts. But remember the decentralized structure of Web 2.0, driven by users' wants and needs and behavior patterns, and use it for good: your good.

Out there in the social media world, of course you are visiting the relevant blogs—or at least those you know about; there are likely more. You can find the blogs in your category by going to Google Reader, an RSS reader [www.google.com/reader], or by going to Freeblogfinder.com. Set up your own RSS feed to watch the blog posting each day; that way you'll be sure to know who is speaking to your audience, who they are listening to, on a moment to moment basis.

One thing I must emphasize: The Internet is a real "do unto others" kind of place. *Never* go in with an overt "sell." *Never* make worthless comments or postings just to get your site listed. That kind of thing backfires; this community will shun you, will shut you out. Go instead with your best ideas, your best comments, and you will quickly establish a reputation as a pro and bring people to you.

Content Sharing

Now this is a fact: You can go to search terms in many categories, including very popular searches, and put them into your search engine, and among the top searches in a very competitive category you will find links taking you back to MySpace, to Facebook, to Squidoo, to Propeller, and to other social media and content-sharing sites.

To bring people to you, get your content out there to them as well. There are so many easy and effective ways to do this. Internet marketer Howie Schwartz says that he hasn't bought a domain, set up a Web hosting account, created a Web site in years. Everything that he does—and he makes his living at it—is in the big wide world of Web 2.0. If he needs a page, he sets it up in Squidoo, in HubPages, in Propeller (see the Resources at the end of this book). He gets entire pages, often page one, of search rankings from his pages. He delights in showing how he outranks the large companies in his categories or product areas—the ones with "crusty old domains" from the 1990s, who haven't yet learned the principles of Web 2.0.

So now it can be your turn. Start by going to www.squidoo.com and putting together your lens—a page featuring your particular point of view or area of expertise—or a group of lenses. The format is there, there is no programming required. Just put in an article (say 500 to 800 words), drop in a few pictures, add a short video, and even put in a poll (people love to participate). All this you can do within the context of the lens template.

Then go to www.hubpages.com and put up a hub (similar to a lens) or two, using the available tools. Make your pages, your hubs, really chock full of content, very useful. For that log home magazine, do "how to find a log home," "how to choose a log home," "how to build a log home." Write a page on how to meet other log home people, how to decorate your log home, where to find resources for your log home. These pages are like mini magazine articles. What a great opportunity to get them out on the Internet!

A really effective strategy for content-sharing sites involves putting up a main hub or lens on a somewhat general topic, for example, "brew your own beer." Then begin to build out sub-pages on related topics: "beer flavors," "sharing recipes," "selling your brand"—whatever relevant information your audience needs, with the secondary pages linking back to your main page. As you continue to post, you get more credibility, presence, and visibility on these sites.

You can put in links to your site here, to your home page or deeper content pages. Put in links to other relevant sites as well, as all of these content sharing sites are looking for impartiality, or at least a healthy appearance thereof. Don't link every single article to your main page or site—that will give the appearance of a link farm. Link some of the pages to your main editorial site, some to a product site, some to your blogs.

You will start to collect readers; you will start to collect fans. Really. You can point them to your blog, your Facebook page, your Web site; you will start getting noticed everywhere.

Really, are the content-sharing strategies that we're using on the Internet so different from all the years, stretching back in the history of magazine publishing, when we got radio spots, TV spots, sent out useful articles to the trade and consumer press about what is hot right that day? Is it so different from the days you used to walk through your supermarket and hear John Mack Carter giving the tip of the week? Not at all. It's the exact same thing—only so much more accessible; so much less costly.

It's best to submit regularly. The sites themselves like to see you post several times a week, but with a once-a-week post you'll soon build a good basis of searchable content out there.

Google has developed a platform called Google Co-op. It allows Internet users to create search engines customized to their own interests. It is possible to submit content for customized search. Simply going in and tagging your content with appropriate labels will get you very targeted rankings for competitive search terms in Google Co-op.

Some publishers have asked me isn't this competing with their own site. The answer, of course, is no. It's getting your own site more widely seen, more widely read, and bringing more people in to it. It's also establishing more links to your site and driving its page rank up in the search engine listings.

If you have the resources to do this, I recommend you hire an Internet editor just to spend all day creating content for the Internet, posting it, and entering discussions and forums. Let the person use his or her own name or a consistent "handle" from site to site; or let the editor use the name of someone at your company who already has a name out there and maybe wants it seen more. He or she will become known, liked, and trusted among that very portion of your audience that spends its time in forums, on social networking sites, and reading blogs—the people you want as participants at your site. It will be a tremendous asset.

Of course you'll want to put articles on Ezine.com and other sites as well. Find out too what sites specialize in your content, and post there.

Even better, of course, than free content sites at which anyone can post are the sites that take submissions based on the merit of the piece and its relevance to the audience. But the free sites bring presence, links, and search rankings as well.

All this is not to say that magazine publishers should abandon their domains and just get out there and mingle. It is to say, however, that the principles of Web 2.0, specifically in this case the content-sharing sites, are only ignored at your peril. If you are not out there rubbing elbows, others are. They are listening, learning, speaking, being heard. They are putting up a page and getting immediate rankings; they are creating content which is indexed and listed within minutes. They are gaining listings that appear above those of sites that have labored for years to establish and maintain rankings.

Don't Let Them Eat Your Lunch

One thing to remember as you bring your material out to these sites: Don't just cut and paste. The content you bring out from your site to the world of Web 2.0 has to be fresh. That doesn't mean that the basic coverage needs to be radically different. But whatever goes out needs to be, at the very least, a rewrite.

Don't just take an article from your site or your blog and put it up as a lens. You can reuse newsletter content, of course, but then you're already doing that on your blog, aren't you?

Taking the same content and posting it all over the Internet can backfire. In the short or the long run, it can endanger your search rankings. Google and the other search engines take duplicate content seriously. The goal of the search engines is to deliver fresh and relevant content to people. Duplicate content endangers search engine relevancy and customer satisfaction.

Many Internet marketing experts believe that search engine spiders identify and discount duplicate content. They assert that as soon as your duplicate content is placed on the Web, that content is recognized and discounted by the spiders and your relevance is lost.

Search expert Jerry West of StomperNet says otherwise. Search engine spiders, he explains, identify duplicate content only internally—from within your own site. Duplicate content found elsewhere on the Internet is still indexed; the search engines do not discover and penalize it.

However, the search spiders are supported by people—thousands of them, who are reviewing searches and assessing results continually. They can and do find duplicate content; in fact, it is one of their mandates to do so.

Additionally, your own competitors are likely to be keeping an eye on what you do. After all, you are watching them, aren't you? If any of your strategies are borderline or questionable, they may not go unnoticed—or unreported.

The penalties for making a false move in your Internet strategy can include loss of search ranking that you have worked years to get, or at least the waste of your efforts in posting content. It makes more sense just to learn to follow best practices for these matters, and one standard best practice is to find or create new content to put up on external sites

Here's where the content-sharing sites themselves make it easy: You only have to read their rules and guidelines to identify best practices.

Titles and Tagging

Remember, at all these content-sharing and other sites you are also going to be creating tags to identify your content. The tags help the search engines find your stuff. A new article, with good keywords and tags, might result in almost immediate spidering by Google and Yahoo.

Tagging is not hard, and the sites will sometimes give you guidelines to work with. Your tags should be short, descriptive, and essentially capture the likely search terms or keyword phrases. Tags should be memorable. To the extent you can use single words do so, over two or three word terms.

Some sites have an algorithm where more tags dilute the ranking of the keywords used; so don't go over a half dozen or so.

In addition to using your own keywords for your tags, as you post new content daily on various content-sharing sites and blogs, you can use the tags relevant to your subject area that are currently searched, currently popular. You can keep tags fresh and current for all newly posted content by scanning news stories, RSS feeds, and social-bookmarking sites.

Visit [http://technorati.com/tag]. Here you'll find today's tags by popularity, showing what people are searching that day—and that hour. You can also visit [http://del.icio.us] to check what is hot today under your specific subject matter. (These tips, by the way, will help you not only with your tagging practices but also may give you ideas for directions to go with your blog postings as well).

There are a few small tips to remember when titling your articles. Just as you do on your site, use your keywords and keyword phrases in your hub titles, your page titles. Just as you do on your magazine cover, get to the point at once without being overly cute or clever.

Get the keyword or phrase into the beginning of the title. That's where the search engines will best pick it up. For example, rather than saying "10 Things You Can Do to Lose Weight in Time for the Holidays" you could say: "Lose Weight: 10 Things You Can Do in Time for the Holidays."

HubPages offers these bits of advice:

Avoid the negative: "What you don't know about kindergarten." People are not searching for a "don't know" phrase.

Avoid using your name, until you are a celebrity. People are not searching for "Jane Doe's Recipes."

Avoid using overly general terms. "Tips" is too broad; add appropriate qualifiers.

Avoid using phrases that reach so far toward cuteness that they have no meaning. (Example: "a tisket, a tasket"—what does that mean?).

Stay away from titles that take too long to get to the point—the search engines will cut you off at 60 characters.

Instead go for phrases searched, words and phrases relevant to your audience.

It sounds as if the newsstand browser and the Internet surfer have a lot in common, don't they? Best practices for titles and tagging will be very familiar to any publishers that has spent much time creating strong and effective cover lines for their magazines.

Social Bookmarking

If you don't already know who they are, take a little time to search for the sites that bookmark pages in your interest category; and of course select a few of the general-interest social-bookmarking sites and start participating. You can start with Digg, StumbleUpon, and Del.icio.us, for example.

This is not something you need to spend masses of time on. It is something, however, that can bring you up in search rankings, like the other social media techniques I've mentioned. The social-bookmarking sites, like the others, tend to show up high in searches across a range of subject matter.

Visit these sites, register, and start "digging," "stumbling," and whatnot. Make some friends; bookmark noncompetitive sites or pages that have value in your subject area and in other, related subject areas.

As on the other sites discussed here, you can't just point everything to your site or sites. To build credibility, bookmark other things of value as well.

By visiting these sites and developing your own list of subjects and connecting to people with similar interests, you also might "stumble upon" something new and relevant in your category.

The goal is not always to be on the first page. Don Crowther of StomperNet mentioned that to be on the first page of Digg can be as much a negative as a positive—those users can't wait to gang up on you. But he has observed that even one "digg" of your site can result in search engine listings.

So go ahead and digg your site, or get someone else to; stumble upon it; give it a thumbs up.

Of course you'll be sure that you are not completely trashing your credibility by bookmarking a sales page, a squeeze page, or a conversion page. If you are going to bookmark anything—you know this by now—it has to have real value.

What has value? An online tool or tutorial; a best/worst list; news or new product information; a great piece of art; a new online booklet of patterns or home plans. These are all the kinds of things that can (should) go into your blog posts, so selectively pointing to blog posts is a great idea. And as you bring people there, of course, you convert them to participants.

One bit of advice (and it's based on another mistake I've seen publishers make) is to stick to a few sites—a few social-media sites, a few content-sharing sites, a few social-bookmarking sites—and really develop a voice and a presence there. Don't try to be all things to all people. Spend some time getting to know what sites are most relevant to your field and your audience, and then bring your considerable resources to becoming a vital, an indispensable part of them.

Video and Photo Sharing

Of course I haven't even spoken about YouTube yet, the elephant in the room. According to Comscore, in December 2007 10 billion videos were watched in the US. That same month 141 million people watched online video. E-Marketer tells us that 52 percent of all Web traffic is video.

Do a few searches in a variety of markets and chances are that something on YouTube will come up pretty high on the results pages. The key point to remember here: Search engines love video.

Video spiders quickly—in only a few minutes in some cases.

Video ranks high—knocking out text-only content for comparable keyword phrases.

You can play your video on a search engines results page.

In short, if you have video on your site, video on your hub pages, video on your blog, you will improve your search rankings significantly.

That is so important, let me say it again: *Video improves search rankings. Significantly.*

Let me say something about making a video and posting it on YouTube: It's not that difficult.

You can, if you want, spend a lot of money to do a high-quality video with expensive cameras, all the right lighting, and professional scripting. If you have a studio set up at your office, or someone you're contracting with to come in and record your videos, you're good to go. You'll probably get a great video to post and, if the topic is appealing and the audience wide enough, you'll get traffic from it.

Or if you want to start quick and dirty, for less than $100 you can buy a Webcam, put it on your computer, and start recording. Just speak a few words into it—words that are of great importance to your audience, words that they will want to hear—and upload it to your account at YouTube, and you will get search listings and traffic from that. If you want to go a little better, you can set up a simple backdrop and a set of video lights and improve the professional appearance of the video in a stroke.

In the world of Internet video, there are people who have very high-end, slick, professional videos now who started only a few months or a year ago with no more than what I've listed above. And then there are people with well-known video blogs and large followings who still use only the most basic equipment and technology mentioned here.

What should you record? You can start with tips. Remember what I said about "how to"—one of the most searched phrases on the Internet? It can just be you or one of your editors talking into a camera—that's a video. Or you can add computer screen captures—power point slides, patterns, screen shots of Web sites or video games, diagrams, beautiful pictures, a photo slide show—whatever is appropriate. Camtasia is the software most used for this on PCs—it's inexpensive and easy to use.

Your video should be brief, no more than about three minutes long. That's the standard, that's what people have grown to expect, and you can cover a lot in three minutes. As time goes by and your following becomes increasingly dedicated, you can increase the length of your videos and use them for other purposes. For a start, and as part of your campaign to bring traffic to your site, three minutes is ample.

A lot of video sites won't let you post your URL in the videos. What you can do is have the Web address, without the .com extension, posted clearly on the last screen of your video. Some people have two versions of their videos—one for their own blog and those sites that allow the URL, and another for the sites that don't. For the sites that do allow a URL, some publishers do a bottom third under the video which includes their domain name for the duration of the video.

In order to accommodate the different video sharing site requirements as well as different test responses, it makes sense to save your video in several different formats, including "with" and "without" the URL, and auto-play versus "click here."

You'll need a keyword-rich title for the video, 64 characters or less. You'll need to make sure that your description also includes your keywords and is 200 words or less. Of course you'll include your full URL in your description along with other relevant contact information (such as a toll-free phone number). Your URL will usually be posted as an active link.

Include a call to action. "For more tips on log home building, visit LogHomeMasterBuilders". "We've shown you here how to make Spaghetti Jubilee. For thousands more pasta recipes, visit PastaMakers."

Of course your URL will also be part of the description tag of the video when it is posted.

Where to post it? On your blog, of course, so it gets into the RSS feeds, and perhaps also on some of your content sharing pages. You can also use a free service such as TubeMogul or a paid one such as Traffic Geyser to release your video to a dozen or more video-sharing sites at once.

PART THREE

What to Do With Them When They Get There

YOUR INTERNET MARKETING *is going to be an integrated, interconnected whole, where each aspect of your marketing effort supports the others, and the end goal is increasing your presence and monetizing your site.*

There are all sorts of aspects to this marketing, though, and they have all sorts of different names. We'll take a look at each of them individually, and in doing so get an idea of some of the creative things that Internet marketers are doing these days.

But first, let's take a look back at everything you know about successful print marketing. Which of these techniques are among the already tested, tried and true tactics of Internet marketing?

Chapter Nine

Copywriting: Dead or Alive?

At least one or two people most active in Internet marketing today have proclaimed that copywriting is dead. The Internet, they say, is not direct mail. It is not a whole lot of other things either—not a lot of other ways that we're used to communicating with our audience. It isn't publishing, that's for sure, and it isn't TV or radio, though it has some of that in it; it isn't image advertising, much too interactive for that, and it isn't—but you get the point.

What the Internet really offers, these people say, is the closest thing to face to face contact that we have seen since the days that salesmen walked from door to door and rat-a-tat-tatted. Once again, you speak directly to people, you can customize your message, you can give them exactly what they are looking for (including the free gift). You can do it interactively, and yes, with video conferencing available and now widely used, you can do it virtually face to face as well.

That still doesn't get it for me. If the Internet is not TV, if it isn't publishing or direct mail, it isn't face to face either. What it offers is a medium whereby you can appeal to individuals in your potential audience in whatever ways they prefer, or in a combination of ways; and this gives Internet marketing a great deal of its power.

By speaking with your audience through print, audio, and video, and interactively through polls, forums and surveys, through games and other social media, you engage more parts of the brain, gaining more of their full attention, and as a result they are likely to be more open to your message and far more engaged with your product.

So the various disciplines of Internet marketing have to do with the various ways in which we engage the audience, the various ways people want to receive information, learn, interact. We interact with them through email, appropriate for those who still structure their days around their inboxes. We interact with them through RSS feeds, for those who like to browse, surf, and pick up tidbits of news. We interact with them through podcasts for those who are more oriented to a portable learning environment, and through mobile feeds for those who want bits on the fly. We interact with those who look for community, for participation, for entertainment, through all the social-networking options available on the Internet.

And a vital, an indispensable part of that interaction still comes through the medium of sales letters.

In fact, of all the resources, paid and free, offered by the so-called "Internet gurus," all the classes, seminars, and things-you-must-know-for-Internet-success that are out there, a very large percentage has to do with good old-fashioned copywriting.

Copywriting is in fact very much alive and well on the Internet. Scan the Internet even casually and you will see long-form sales letters; short-form sales letters; call outs; P.S.'s; Johnson boxes—all the features of direct mail copywriting applied to Web marketing.

Let's take a few moments to review some of the necessary elements of copywriting as it applies to your Web site and to all of your marketing copy, whether spoken or written:

Know Your Audience

This has always been the beginning, the basis of all successful marketing. Who are you speaking to—and what do they want? What are their greatest pains, needs, wants, desires, aspirations? What are they truly looking for?

Considering the market research you've been doing with keywords, you've already made a brilliant start with this. Keyword research is the fastest, cheapest way there has ever been to find out what is really on people's minds. A keyword tracker can show you the top searches of the past month, for example—all the top searches, or the top searches in your category, or for your keyword clusters.

This is a market researcher's dream: a fast, easy search, which is cheap or free, to discover what people are looking for, in the very words they are looking for it. How many focus groups would you give for that kind of information?

There is another step you can take, using the Google AdWords tracking tool, that shows not only what people are interested in but also whether they are spending any money on it. So there you have it, steps one and two: find out what are people searching for, find out what are they spending money on.

But there are other steps to take. All great marketers will advise you to go beyond the first level of desire to find out what underlies it. "I want a log home" might translate to "I want to have a nifty unique place to show off to my friends," or it might translate to "I want to get cozy with my family in a home that makes me feel safe, as if I'm going back in time." It's important to understand which it is before beginning the dialog with the potential customer.

That emotional benefit, though, tracks back to an even deeper desire: the desire to feel good about oneself. So "I want a unique place to show my friends" might track back to "I feel good about myself because I'm a trend-setter, someone who doesn't follow the latest thing," or "because I have great taste"; the desire for a cozy haven might track back to "I feel good about myself because I nurture my family, I take care of them;" and of course in almost any category you will at times track back to "because it makes me more appealing to the opposite sex."

In order to sell anything effectively, you have to know what desire is really being expressed, and then you have to speak directly to that desire. So you are selling, not the stacked timber of the log walls, not even the safe haven or cozy getaway, but the end goal of feeling good about the way I nurture my family.

So the first step of copywriting is, and has been for all time, to learn about what makes the customer, the audience, the participant tick.

Never has it been easier. Now instead of expensive mailings or focus groups that are limited in reach—or in addition to those still-useful tools—you can put a survey up on the Internet, drive some people to it through pay-per-click advertising, or from your blog, or through your email list, and you will quickly get useful, actionable answers.

Essentially, the Internet has revolutionized this first, fundamental step of great marketing. Our there on the Internet, you are part of your market. You are blogging with it, participating in forums with it, participating with it on social bookmarking sites, swapping content, collecting user-generated content. There are so many ways to pull information in from your audience, to be a fly on the wall, an ear to the ground, a sympathetic friend with whom to share.

Internet marketers are finding that within a very short period of time, the space of a few days or weeks, they can discover the most pressing needs and wants of their market, create a product, and launch that product into a market that has just requested it.

By the way, surveys themselves are, to a certain age group and demographic, of themselves something worthy of forwarding, and a properly worded survey can not only increase your understanding of your market and its needs but even further build your lists.

Speak to One Person, Not to Many

Eben Pagan, known among Internet marketers for coining the phrase "move the free line," calls it "creating a customer avatar": developing and envisioning a personification, essentially, of the person to whom you are selling. But of course this is the exercise that direct mail copywriters have been using forever to enable them to write copy that is fresh, immediate, natural, and intimate in tone.

Is your customer a twenty-something male who uses the latest technology to keep in touch with his friends and stay ahead of the curve at the office, who wants of all things for his boss to recognize his brilliance and his girlfriend to wilt in awe? Is it a working mother who is distressed that she doesn't spend enough time with her children and wants some kind of assurance that she's doing the best job of parenting anyone could ever do? Give the customer a name, an age, imagine what your customer looks like, feels like. Identify what it is that person wants most of all.

Frank Kern, another successful Internet marketing entrepreneur who has also had great success in selling information products to vertical markets, says "what my audience wants is to sit at their computer doing nothing and having money just spewing out of it at them. So I have to give them what I can that comes closest to what they want."

So create your avatar, the personification of the group of people that are your customers, and speak directly to that person when you are writing your Internet marketing copy.

Greater Targeting is More Effective Than Greater Generalization

For years, magazine publishers have understood the importance of narrowing down your focus to the point where audience members can actually feel as if you are speaking directly to them.

If I am trying to drive traffic, or as we now say, to bring people to the Web site of a health magazine, for example, I don't want to just say "feel better." True, everyone wants to feel better, why not? But it is so broad and general that it ends up speaking to no one. It's better to address people exhausted by insomnia, and promise that they can browse your site for tips on sleeping better, or target the person who needs to lose those last ten pesky pounds, offering strategies to do just that.

The difference? Today you can segment your lists with demographic and psychographic information as never before. Through tracking customer preferences in Web browsing, through creating market segments based on keyword groups searched, through dividing lists based on specific opt-in request groups, through simple customer surveys, you can create ever more targeted lists, and test different kinds of sales copy and approaches to the separate list segments.

It's Not About You, It's About Them

Not only in your marketing materials but on your site itself, this principle will serve you well. People do not visit your site to find out about you. They are not really interested in your history, your mission, your slogan, your location, what your corporate offices look like. They are interested in what you can do for them.

How will you change their lives, solve their problems, make them smarter, better-looking, healthier, richer? That's the reason they come to your site. It's also why they read your blog—not to hear about the new offices you're moving into or what you had for breakfast.

Bear in mind that the personal details do have a role to play in developing relationships, creating intimacy and a common bond. Used for that purpose it can enhance your marketing efforts and increase the return. But use that kind of thing wisely and consciously. For the most part, when people read your marketing or arrive at your site, what should meet them is not a statement of how great you are, but how they will find what they need. Don't even tell them what you will teach them; tell them what they will learn.

Again, this is an approach that the Internet has brought to more advanced levels than we could previously dream. Just think about how Amazon has created an individualized store, by name, for every customer visiting its site. To click onto that site you immediately find, not what Amazon has done to sell other customers that day, but what it has selected as items of interest to you personally.

When a magazine publisher creates a site based on the needs of its visitors, it generates a loyalty in the audience otherwise inconceivable. Visit *The Old Farmer's Almanac* Web site [www.almanac.com] and discover why, with its weather updates specific for it visitors and its unique bits of trivia and historical data, many people use it as their own browser home page. What a strong connection that fosters between publisher and audience!

Establish Your Unique Selling Proposition

This concept has been around since the 1940s and is as relevant and necessary today on the Internet as it has been in every other form of sales and marketing.

Your unique selling proposition, or USP, is what distinguishes you from other sites in your category and/or sites offering similar products. An oft-cited example is Domino's Pizza: Lots of local places will deliver your pizza, but Domino's will get it to you in just 30 minutes—or it's free.

Here as elsewhere magazine publishers are way ahead of the game. In creating the concept and content for their publication they have already developed a clear idea of just what it is that distinguishes them from other publications, what appeals to their particular audience, and what makes them special to that audience.

Say, for example, you are a guitar magazine publisher. You already know your USP: You know that of the many guitar magazines out there, yours is the only one offering a dozen transcripts, or catering to the advanced student, or featuring Hendrix every issue. You hear from your readers issue after issue telling you why they love you more than any other title in the category.

Whatever your actual publication, make sure your USP is clearly stated and known to marketing and design people, and you're good to go.

Emphasize Benefits, Not Features

This marketing principle, well established from the very early days when marketing was becoming seen as a science, is applicable to many more things than just your direct mail packages. Working with publishers on their magazine covers, I tell them to go for the benefit, not the feature. Don't tell me that you have found six new places to go, tell me that you have found six secret getaways. Don't tell me about the diet, tell me about the weight I will lose. Never forget that the reader wants to know "what's in it for me?"

Can you think of any reason this important, well understood, tried and true principle would be any different in your Internet marketing or on your Web site itself than it is in any other context? I can't.

So don't tell your audience that you have listings, tell them they will find resources. Don't tell them that you are offering six issues of your magazine, but that you will deliver to them the latest and most useful information that will help them become a better guitar player, mountaineer, yoga practitioner, or what have you—six times a year.

Use Testimonials

One thing that everyone looks for when planning on making any sort of commitment of time, money, or resources—and you are likely to be asking your site visitor to commit these things—is social proof. Social proof can be defined as the seal of approval that the group gives a product or service that makes it more acceptable and desirable to other members of the group.

There are a lot of ways of developing social proof. One way is through the social marketing discussed in previous chapters—first become part of the group, then give helpful information, and attain a position of authority and respect. A Web site with millions of visitors has lots of social proof. Lively participation in your forums and contributions to your blogs by respected, known, or just plain interesting and smart individuals is another way to gather social proof.

And one way that is hard to beat is testimonials. The best testimonials, of course, are from other industry experts, other figures of authority that your audience knows, likes, and trusts. Testimonials from happy satisfied site participants, product users, seminar attendees are great, too.

If you offer something free on your blog—an information video, access to a new piece of software or Web application, a funny or entertaining video—and the first people to respond to it do so gratefully and enthusiastically, that's great social proof, and it helps shape the way other people respond to what you are offering.

The great thing about testimonials online is that they can be in various formats—transcript, audio, video—to appeal to different parts of the site participant's brain and increase the level of credibility, authority, and authenticity of the testimonial.

So litter your site with them; lard your marketing pieces with them. Record short ones in video and post them on your site. Use them to support every product you offer.

Employ the Principle of Scarcity

Almost every really successful product offering uses scarcity in some way or another: "Act now while supplies last"; "Only good until Thursday midnight"; "We only have phone lines available for the first 500 callers"; "Special rate good until the 30th"—and so on.

You've used it on your direct mail, you've used in almost everything you've ever done. Look at Internet marketing offers and you'll see it is equally the norm here.

Frank Kern seems to take a mischievous delight in employing scarcity while using a colloquial and earnest tone to claim not to. (The pitch goes something like this: I'm not going to start doing the whole scarcity thing, but you need to know that 20,000 people have signed up for my list since yesterday, and I'm only going to have 500 places, because I want everyone in my course to get the level of attention they deserve.) Other marketers claim they will release a certain secret knowledge once—then never again, no matter who begs them to do so.

Like any good marketing technique, scarcity has to be used in a believable and compelling way to be effective. Like any good marketing technique, used in a rote or repetitive fashion it will quickly lose impact. But when used as a carefully applied element of an overall sales push, it remains a powerful tool in the marketer's toolbox.

Give Away Lots of Bonuses

Here's another area where the power and flexibility of the Internet makes the use of a long-standing marketing element ("How much would you pay for this? But WAIT! There's more...") easier and more cost-effective to implement than ever before.

In standard sales and marketing, bonuses are a powerful way to increase purchases and reduce refunds—but they add significant costs to the process of selling. In magazine retail sales, adding a premium to the product can increase sales ten, twenty percent or more. Even with these increases, magazine publishers can often not afford the cost of creating and printing another information product and bagging it onto the magazine.

In cyberspace, the bonuses offered are usually information products, *and*—this is the key—the information products are usually *downloadable*.

This means that the addition of bonuses to the offer of a product, service, or launch is both inexpensive and almost infinitely scalable.

Internet marketers use bonuses to add to the benefit of an offer. Their affiliates use bonuses to encourage the purchase of a product through their particular channel. Bonuses offered are often assigned a value equal to or greater than the price asked for the product, service, or launch. Bonuses are thrown in as a surprise feature subsequent to a purchase as a way of keeping customer satisfaction high, increasing customer loyalty, and minimizing requests for refunds.

Bonuses are also used in conjunction with the scarcity principle to trigger early sales. "First 500 people to sign on to this information seminar get this audio course valued at $500 FREE."

Downloadable information products used for bonuses can be ebooks, audio or video series, free membership—for a limited time—in a membership site or mastermind group, free group consulting for a limited time, a series of conference calls, even something as simple and scalable as a collection of video clips pulled from YouTube ("We scoured the Internet for the very funniest home video clips and give them to you FOR FREE in return for your online purchase of Home Video magazine…").

For a more expensive, higher-value video training program, an Internet marketer might offer as a bonus a free day or weekend attendance at a conference or seminar. This helps fill the room for a seminar which will then be reused in video format for future information-product offerings. It may be offered for a time after the refund offer has expired; its perceived value is so high that it can reduce refund requests significantly as well as further cementing relationships with customers.

Guarantee Your Product

You've always done this with your subscriptions, haven't you?: full refund for unused portion of the subscription; full refund for entire subscription; for more daring, or confident publishers, a full refund for the entire subscription may be made available until the very last issue.

It's called reversing the risk, and its purpose is to help overcome sales resistance. Marketers know that once that resistance is overcome the percentage of requests for refunds will be low. The principle of reciprocity states that if customers get real value from something purchased, they are unlikely to ask for their money back.

Indeed, the more generous your refund offer is, paradoxically, the fewer refund requests you are likely to get. For a 30-day refund offer, customers might be careful to be aware of the deadline, evaluate the benefit, weigh the outcome. For a lifetime refund offer, the pressure is off. The focus turns from the idea of asking for a refund to the idea of getting the most out of the product.

As your price point goes up, of course, the steps you take to minimize refund requests should get more aggressive. The more you develop your relationships with your audience, the more those requests decline. So get them involved in your forums and blogs, answer their questions, honor their ideas. Turn to them for content. Ask them for testimonials. A customer who has offered a testimonial is engaged. Once they have spoken in your favor, they are unlikely to ask for a refund.

Always Include a Call to Action

The long-standing direct mail principle of the call to action is well known yet astoundingly still sometimes forgotten, ignored, or otherwise honored only in the breach. Yet on the Internet, the call to action principle can reach complete fulfillment. Here the call, the action, and the result can be virtually instantaneous.

Virtually every Web site on the Internet today is completely loaded with calls to action, though many Web site owners and users do not recognize them as such. What are they? They are the clickable links which lace every page of every site. And while these links might not always be the true calls to action of the marketing world, they are at the very least *invitations* to action. They invite the site participant to take a specific action—to click a link—which will yield a specific result: more information, an opt-in list, perhaps just a change of scene.

What both the site designer and the marketer must keep in mind are what actions are being offered and what the results of those actions might be. Why is the link on the page? Is it to build traffic to another site, to other pages within the site? Is the purpose to add value to the site participant, to add to the level of information the site offers, or to increase another page's link value? Or is the link being offered, the invitation to action, a complete distraction, an utter waste?

In the case of conversion pages, "squeeze" pages, or places where you are calling to an action that will result in some kind of opt-in, whether monetized or otherwise, focus on that call. Minimize or eliminate other invitations to action.

Not long ago there was a theory of Internet commerce: your page should be geared to conversion, period. The goal was to get people to come, get people to buy, and if they didn't want to buy, let them go away. Briefly summarized: come and buy or go away.

There is still a certain sense to this theory for some kinds of sites or, within a site, some kinds of pages. In particular the purpose of a conversion page is to convert the browser to an ongoing participant of some kind. The entire page should be that specific kind of call. There shouldn't be subordinate links leading off to other pages of the site, or to other kinds of information not relevant to the action of the opt-in. The call for action should be simple, clear, and compelling. This is something we'll talk about more in chapter eleven.

Chapter Ten
Is Branding Dead? (No It Isn't)

As any magazine publisher knows, branding has certainly been the big deal. We don't speak of publications, or titles, or magazines anymore; we speak of *brands*. We don't look at building an audience, we look at "building the brand."

Particularly now as our publications extend out beyond the print platform, the concept of "the brand" makes sense: It is simply taking the editorial voice, the editorial mission, and the the minute-by-minute engagement of the relationship with the readers and extending it across all platforms, regardless of medium.

In the Internet world, however, you will find some level of disenchantment with the concept of branding, and there is a certain amount of sense in this, too. Branding, in the view of many Internet marketers, is synonymous with image advertising: writing songs and jingles to brand Coke versus Pepsi, or spending maybe a few billion dollars to get the Nike swoosh imprinted in the popular imagination.

That kind of scattershot approach, which requires millions of dollars to create millions of impressions, whose ultimate end is questionable (will the brand take hold? Will the approach be appealing? Will it result in sales? Will the sales result in profit?) is seen as old marketing, old thinking, irrelevant in the fast-moving, highly targeted world of Internet sales.

The brand, it is argued, is not important. People do not search by brand. People search by keyword, they come to a site that promises to deliver on the purpose of the search term, and they stay on the site or leave the site based on whether or not it meets their needs, regardless of brand.

There's truth to that—though it's interesting to me to watch many of these same Internet marketers working so hard to brand themselves among their audience as "the guru of Internet marketing," "the guru of gurus," "the maven marketer," "the authoritative voice," and so on. And to a good degree it works. Each so-called guru grabs a spot in the market with a particular form of marketing savvy and gets his or her name attached to it, and gets support from the other gurus in the world of Web 2.0 as well.

So even in a world that professes to have grown beyond branding, branding exists. Branding is big.

There are lessons to be learned, instructive points to be made in the branding-versus-no-branding debate. The first comes back to the classic marketing concept: it's not about you, it's about them.

We exist online to meet the needs of the people there. And it is very, very easy, deadly easy, for them to shift elsewhere if what we offer doesn't hit the mark. Fortunately, it also is pretty easy to keep them there if it does.

In the world of the Internet, it tends to be the newbies who are doing searches. They are the ones typing "how can I get a date" or "how can I develop my abs" or "how can I teach my parrot to talk" into the search engine windows and then navigating to the top sites the search engines offer up.

The experts in a given field tend to already know where they want to go. They are not doing the searches per se; they are hanging out on the content network. They have their favorite sites, favorite groups, favorite forums, and they visit there to talk to their friends, discuss the latest products, weigh in on the issues, and get all the news and tips and information.

Your goal is to bring in the former and convert them to the latter. In the world of magazine publishing, it's called audience development. It's about connecting along the maximum number of points, at the maximum number of times throughout the day and week and month and year. "The brand" here is so much more than your logo, or sub tag, or page design. It is you being part of the life of your audience, and your audience being part of the life of your publication, your Web site, your videos and audios and podcasts. Your brand is nothing less than your voice, your mission, your entire relationship with your audience.

Chapter Eleven

Tools, Techniques, and Best Practices

There are so many marketing tools available online, it is no wonder that various forms of marketing have sprung up, each with their own set of principles, each with their own set of gurus.

I wouldn't call them schools of marketing, however. What the various kinds of Internet marketing represent in reality is a complete set of best practices that are continually being developed, refined, and revised as audience desires, needs, and expectations evolve in the fast-changing online environment. As new tools are developed, new marketing ideas are introduced, tested, evaluated, and taught.

Probably since the early part of the twentieth century, when direct marketers were first beginning to portray themselves as artists and scientists and to formulate approaches that they tested and proved (many of them covered in chapter 9 above), there has never been such an exciting, dynamic time for marketers. Probably it wasn't even as heady then, actually, as it is now, when new ideas can be conceived, tested, and implemented so inexpensively, so quickly, and with so little risk; and results can be analyzed and quantified and assigned a monetary value; and there is such a hungry audience for the ideas developed and the knowledge gained.

And every day there is something new! A new tool, application, widget, or template, or a piece of software that offers connections or ease of use or visibility undreamed of in the not-too-distant past. Yesterday you hired a programmer to start a blog. Today you go to WordPress and download a template—free! Yesterday you took college-level courses to learn HTML programming; today you grab a users manual, set up a template, and go. Yesterday you spent years and tens or hundreds of thousands of dollars to set up a social media site; today you go to Ning and it's done.

What this means for publishers and for marketers is that there are more ways to reach our audience, and more things we can do for them, than ever before; more than we had ever previously imagined. What's more, thanks to the efforts of the many great marketers in this field, sets of best practices have been formulated and are evolving and can be used as guidelines for publishers looking to develop a clear and coherent roadmap for building their audience and monetizing their online presence.

And the start and end and crux of it all, of course, is:

Free Stuff

The name of the Internet game is getting information for free, and that doesn't look as if it's going to change any time soon. It's been well documented in our industry's press how publishers who started with a free model got out of the gate fast, and those publishers looking to monetize through selling or setting up other barriers to obtain content were left behind.

By now Internet users are well used to getting what they seek for free, and they know that if one site doesn't offer it, another will. This posed a nasty problem for publishers in the early days of the Internet, as they poured hundreds of thousands of dollars into developing a Web presence without effective operational plans for getting these sites to pay back.

Don Nicholas withdrew at that time from his core specialization of subscription marketing and spent several years researching best practices on the Internet, discovering just what works for successful publishers. Under the auspices of his consulting company, Mequoda, he formulated a roadmap to Web site monetization for magazine publishers that is based on the very dynamics of the Internet itself: the giving and receiving of information, for free.

Of course Don offers a lot more than just that under Mequoda, and to find it all I would encourage you to visit his Web site and acquaint yourself with him. But the basic concept here, and the one I'll use as my starting point in talking about the approaches to Internet marketing, is about harnessing this fundamental principle of Web use and using it to create, build, and monetize your entire Web business.

Variously called educational marketing, results in advance (RIA), and "moving the free line," the free stuff principle is that people come to the Internet—and to your Web site—to amuse themselves, meet people, and learn things. And if you can give them what they are looking for, you are well on your way to developing a relationship with them. It is your responsibility as a publisher and a Web marketer to make sure that that relationship develops into an ongoing one, and that that ongoing relationship becomes long term, and that when these visitors look to buy more information or other products in your category, it is to you they turn.

You are the publisher. Who better to provide information than you? Someone is looking for that information. That someone is, by definition, a potential audience member for your sites, your publications.

So offer what people are looking for. Answer their questions, do it for free. Give them the opportunity for more free information. Let them opt in to what you have to offer: your newsletter or tips guide or video tutorial. Show them how they will continue to get value as they keep coming to you.

Eben Pagan talks about "moving the free line." Give them your very best ideas up front, he says. Tell them something that, with a few small changes or a minor effort, will change their lives. The shift in grip that will improve their golf swing, the phrase or gesture or smile that will get them the date, the business tip that will net them that much more money that very day. Once you have done that and they try it and it works, they trust you. They want to know more of what you know; they want all the tips that have made you so successful in your area of interest.

Don't hold back, he says. Don't say: Well, if you give me your credit card number now I'll send you that information later. That's not the way to establish trust, not the way to build a relationship. Give it freely, up front. Give more value, more information than anyone could possibly expect. Move the free line here, and then at the other end you can move the paid line as well. Instead of just selling an ebook or special report for nineteen or twenty dollars, you can sell a video seminar for a thousand dollars, or a week long retreat for ten thousand.

Frank Kern talks about RIA, or results in advance. His image is that you want to get to a certain goal—the goal, let's say, of getting freedom from your back pain. If someone starts you down that road—for example, shows you a simple exercise you can do that will ease the chronic pain at least partially, at least briefly—then you see that they know how to reach that goal. You see that they can start you on your way there, and you want to go the rest of the way with them. You've started down the road that leads to the relief of chronic pain, and you've done it for free and gotten good results in advance. You want to go the rest of the way, and now you are willing to pay to do it.

Don Nicholas points out that, as magazine publishers, we have that information. All of it. It is our editorial product and no, we don't just have to post it all online for free.

What we can do, Don tells us (and by the way, he tells us for free) is establish the massive amounts of information in our libraries and archives into minimum information units. If you are the publisher of cooking magazines, the minimum information unit might be a recipe. If you are the publisher of video-gaming magazines, it might be a "cheat"—the shortcut that enables you to get a certain prize or go to another level. For a photography magazine it might be a tip. For an entertainment magazine it could be a celebrity photo, a bit of gossip; for a humor magazine publisher it could be a comic or a joke. These minimum information units (MIUs) become the basis for the freebies you offer your audience.

Send the MIU, the freebie to them as a newsletter. Send it every month, or every week, or every day. As long as your value is there to the reader, more frequency is better than less frequency. It keeps your relationship fresh and your readership appreciative. But many publishers find success with less frequent correspondence as well. And through skillful copywriting, an old list can be brought to life despite former neglect.

Marketers find that a list can tolerate a sales pitch every three or four mailings; so alternate three or so good content releases with a pitch for a for-pay product. However in the context of a value-packed newsletter itself, there can be other offers—of special reports, ebooks, or other information products relevant to the information presented.

A "Sticky" Site Versus a "Buy or Leave" Site

A commonly held theory about conversion marketing is that the purpose of your site is to get the visitor to do what you want or just go away. You have no reason to keep your visitors there, says this school of thought, if they aren't going to take the action you have brought them there to take. They need to sign up for your newsletter, purchase a product, leave a name, click through to another page or another site. Don't distract them, don't pull them away from their purpose or goal.

The approach to Internet publishing—to which this conversion principle stands in opposition—is to create a "sticky" site: one which offers a wealth of content as well as a variety of reasons for visitors to come to the site, to stay on the site, and to return to the site repeatedly. Your site is a destination—your audience comes to visit and stays to hang out.

For magazine publishers, the "sticky" school of thought obviously makes the most sense. Even so, there are pages that should only have one job to do, and they should do it well: These are conversion pages.

Conversion Marketing

All really successful marketing efforts are database driven. A list, a good, responsive, permission-based list, is an essential, unavoidable, irreplaceable part of any marketing plan.

This list becomes the backbone of all efforts.You can start a major marketing effort without a list, but if you do so it is certain that the initial focus of that effort will be the development of a list.

You develop your lists in a number of ways: through blogging, social marketing, viral marketing (we'll get to that shortly), and of course through search engine optimization. The purpose of all these efforts, though, is to drive people to the Web site, to bring them in. Once they are there, the goal is to have them turn into mailable names. The rate at which they do so is your conversion rate.

Your conversion rate, in other words, is the percentage of visitors to your site who take the conversion action: the action that your conversion marketing is geared towards getting visitors to take. The goal here, of course, is to get the highest possible conversion rate.

Conversion marketing, therefore, is the art and science of getting people to take an action that you want them to take. It could be buying a product or filling out a form to get more information. But in the best practices of Internet marketing, conversion is by and large the process of getting the prospect to opt in to your list.

Conversion marketing is the pivot around which all your other marketing efforts turn. The conversion is the moment you turn a casual visitor into an ongoing customer, audience member, a willing ally. Through conversion you swing the entire dynamics of your relationship with your site visitor, creating an ongoing bond which becomes the basis of your future interactions.

Conversion marketing is the engine that drives the entire series of complex, dynamic, and interactive sequences that form the structure of Internet marketing. Conversion has changed the nature of marketing entirely. It has moved it irrevocably from the days of interruption marketing to something entirely new, entirely different, entirely Web based.

"Interruption marketing," the off-line model, is the process of trying to capture a prospect's attention in some way, through a space ad, or billboard, or TV spot, or direct mail; the process of reaching out and screaming, "Hey! Here I am! Pay attention! I have something to sell you!"

And what has interruption marketing become in the universe of interconnectivity, relationships, networks, and choice which is Web 2.0? It's become *permission marketing*: the mutual agreement between you and your prospective customer that you will earn the right to present buying opportunities based on continuous value—the value of information and entertainment that you provide and the consequent value placed by the customer on your relationship.

So here's how it works: you get people to come to your site through a combination of efforts such as those outlined in chapters 4 through 8, and convert them to an opt-in, permission-based mailing list by offering them something they want.

It sounds simple, and in some ways it is. But conversion marketing is a dynamic and ever-changing aspect of your Internet marketing, and one to which you need to pay careful attention.

To begin with, keep in mind that your offer—the free information that you are giving away in exchange for permission to mail—needs to be very valuable to your audience. Gone are the days when a simple "sign up for our free newsletter" would take care of your list-building efforts. People today are bombarded by offers of free newsletters, and there are only so many they will permit to be delivered to their inboxes. Estimates vary from ten to fifteen, and it does depend on a variety of factors, including the frequency with which the enewsletter is sent. But when the limit is reached, people begin canceling. Unless yours is one that is welcomed and read for the content it offers, you can be sure it will be one of the ones that is canceled.

Then, even if your offer is good, your Web site needs to be optimized for conversion. I have worked on sites where the opt-in is buried under "resources" or "take action" or other generic tags; or where it is found below the fold; or where it isn't found on the home page at all.

Every page of your site should include conversion architecture, and the conversion itself should be easy and quick. Just "click here," a first name, an email address, and you will get the maximum number of sign ups. If you begin to ask for too much information, resistance will kick in and conversions will drop.

As part of the conversion architecture, many sites include a so-called (attractively named) *squeeze page*: a page created to facilitate the process of conversion. A squeeze page might include a headline or caption, some sales copy, a call to action, a place for a prospect to leave a name and email address, and nothing more—no navigation links, no irrelevant or strictly editorial information.

As part of the conversion series, a visitor who opts in to a squeeze page might receive an *autoresponder* letter. The letter might confirm the subscription or provide a double opt-in: a request for the visitor to click back through to the Web site to confirm the request for information and follow-up. The purpose of the double opt-in is to protect your list from possible spammers and increase the quality and commitment of your list. The double opt-in does, of course, reduce conversion percentages, and many marketers assert that an autoresponder to the new subscribers explaining why they are getting the email and giving them an easy way to unsubscribe is all that is necessary.

In any case, your sales process can continue right through the autoresponder and double opt-in. You can offer valuable information, links to additional pages, and even options to buy other products or services through these pages.

Your squeeze pages, your autoresponder letters, or the site to which a double opt-in takes someone could also include a video or audio sales message or brief instruction, and some marketers have found these tools to increase conversions up to 40 percent.

All these elements need to be tested, of course. What increases conversions on one site or one squeeze page could reduce them on another.

In fact the very existence of the squeeze page itself should be tested on your site. Some marketers find that just a place on the home page or other landing pages for a visitor to drop a name and email address is enough. Others won't require an opt-in at all with an early offering. These marketers swear by the "reverse squeeze": give the high value gift first, harvest the names after. Let the visitor to the site find something of value—an information-packed video, for example, that they can view with no commitment whatsoever—and they will be eager to give their contact information at the first opportunity. If they are not, these marketers argue, the visitor is not sufficiently targeted to deserve a place on the list.

Whatever your conversion strategy, it is one that should be tested and analyzed on an ongoing basis. Do you harvest the maximum number of names possible and mail and later market to all of them? Or do you screen and target early on, and have the most responsive names on your list? It depends in part on what you are doing with the names, how you are marketing to them, and what the cost is of having them on your list.

Direct Marketing (Email Marketing)

Direct email marketing traces its genesis from old-fashioned direct mail packages, using many of the marketing techniques described in chapter 9, with the goal of selling a subscription or some other product, or getting the email recipient to take some action.

Its beginning, for many publishers, was the transfer of direct mail practices to an email format, and there, for some, it remains. But for most, there has at least begun an evolution in direct marketing techniques to new ways of doing things adapted to cyberspace.

One technique you will hear frequently mentioned is the short form sales letter versus the long form sales letter. Email readers look for shorter letters, says conventional wisdom; and the long form letter is losing its place in email marketing.

Even a cursory look at Internet marketing practices, however, will show you that there are many long form letters being successfully used: in email letters, as landing pages to Web sites, as home pages on Web sites. Don Nicholas asserts that there is still a place for long form letters, "good old fashioned story telling," as he puts it. The more money you ask for, the longer your letter might need to be to make its sell points.

Other marketers concur. "Take as long as you need to tell the story" is a principle that has held true since the early days of direct marketing, and it holds true now, they tell us.

Whether you are using the long form letter or the short term letter, the headline is the most important part of your email. Test various headlines, just as you would in your old direct mail series. Test various subject lines, captions, and headers. If the subject line is compelling, you get people to open the email; if the header of the email is effective, the recipients will read on. If neither is powerful, you've already lost them, and it doesn't matter how good your copy is.

Split every mailing to test two, three, or even more subject lines and headlines. Try new things; compare to what has worked before.

Closely following your headline in importance—and in placement on your email—are the testimonials. Collect testimonials whenever you can and use them liberally in your mailings.

An evolution of the long form letter has appeared in recent email marketing efforts: the division of the old long form sales letter into a marketing series, which is sent sequentially to an opt-in list. This approach—which would have been cost-prohibitive in many cases prior to the development of email marketing—was pioneered by Internet marketer Jeff Walker, who called it the "sideways sales letter." It entails separating the sales letter into sequential parts, beginning for example with a teaser/headline, moving to the story, the proof (examples of success, testimonials, etc.), and on to the offer, the guarantees, the call for action, and so on.

This approach is best implemented using a variety of the Internet communication tools at hand in addition to the email sequence: blogging, posting, offering video shorts, a viral effort, and so on.

It's important to realize that these variations on approaches call on the ingenuity of the Internet marketer to hold the interest of the audience through sequential sales efforts. The story told must be compelling, and each step of the sales process must offer information of value on its own, in order for it to be successful. Otherwise the email recipients will spot it for a marketing effort early on in the sequence and begin to ignore, discount, or discard future efforts.

Think of it as the old Burma Shave sequences by the roadside: Entertain and delight early on in the sequence and the audience will follow it through to the end. Fail to do so and you lose their attention and their interest.

In designing your email marketing sequences, pay attention to what portion of your email will appear in recipients' preview panes. As in so many other contexts, the focus is top left. That's where your teasers, TOCs, or calls to action will go. Don't clog that important upper left with your logo or other branding image—in most cases that branding is not as powerful an impetus to open the email as a different kind of teaser.

One final word on the subject: Make sure to validate the code in your email messages.

Database Marketing

A refinement on the process of email marketing is the related and overlapping process of database marketing, also called targeted marketing, or segmented marketing.

Database marketing implies you have a list—a prerequisite of email marketing. There are Internet marketers who claim to do very well, thank you, without any list at all—primarily through affiliate marketing and driving traffic to their ecommerce sites—but even those marketers usually end up collecting names and building their own lists.

Building a list is a way of smoothing out fluctuations in the market that would have a big impact on search marketing, for example. Are people not searching your keyword terms lately? Did you somehow, for some inexplicable reason, just get slapped by Google, and your page ranking has plummeted as a result? Or perhaps you were pushed off page one for some important search terms by Google 2.0—while images, video, or local directory listings have nudged their way to the top?

No matter. You still have a list. You can still reach your most committed, targeted audience any time you want to.

You can use your database to test new ideas, to survey your market, to announce big news, to draw people's attention to your latest posts or updates. You can use it to launch or market a product.

You can use your list to send broadcast emails to everyone on it: a special report, a bit of news, a limited-time opportunity. In the oft-repeated words of Frank Kern: "Just press 'send' and make money."

You can set your list up with an autoresponder sequence which begins a follow-up series based on the date that a prospect signed up to your list. The autoresponder could be a sequential series of tips or a sales series.

The autoresponder series itself could be set up on a segmented basis, with one series made available to subscribers expressing one set of interests, another for those who have expressed others.

A good series is also adaptable based on the responses of recipients to each email. For example, in a sales series, a flexible database/emarketing provider will continue to mail to the people who have not yet responded to the specific offer made, while dropping the names that have already responded or shifting them to another mailing sequence.

Database marketing is simply a continuation of the process of getting to know your customers. Find out about them, their demographic information, their specific wants and needs, their fears and frustrations, and get that information into your database. Then target your marketing to the specific segments of the group.

A question that might come up is how you can encode all this information into your database if, as part of your conversion effort, you are asking for no more than a name and an email address. If asking for more reduces the conversion rate so dramatically, how do you reconcile the conversion with the database segmenting?

Magazine publishers, however, are starting from the opposite side of the picture when it comes to their databases. In our subscriber files we have regional information, zip code information, demographic information, and psychographic information. We have a picture of the overlapping publications of interest to our audience, the children they are raising, the games they are playing, the businesses they are starting. We know their likes and dislikes.

What we frequently don't have are their email addresses.

Getting those addresses has proved a challenge to some publishers, but not a completely insurmountable one. From "enter online" contests that are offered to subscribers, to subscriber surveys which include requests for email addresses, to telephone surveys, to a simple field added to a subscription card, we've begun to collect this information. And as we gather it we've begun to request and be granted the permission to include our subscribers as part of our email lists. So we enter the field with a quantity of information available on who makes up our lists that would be the envy of many Internet marketers.

As we gather additional names online, there are many ways to collect information even as we keep the conversion sequence simple and effective. Dividing up your information offerings is a great way to start. If you have a travel publication, break out what you are offering and allow your prospective customers to check off which options they would prefer: The tips on family travel? Budget travel? Luxury travel? Spas? Based on what they check off you have a good start on the information you want to collect about your customers.

For the names you collect from your Web marketing efforts, as you build relationships you can ask for more information. Get the names, provide some good value, build trust. Then you can send out a survey, or create a contest, or offer a Web-based application in return for more information.

And of course as your prospects actually buy things from you, you are collecting more complete information from them.

The key, of course, to effective database marketing is an in-house email marketing system or an outsourced email marketing service that is flexible enough to maintain your lists and mail to them on a segmented basis. A good emarketing system will be able to mail in a series (dropping off the names of people who have already responded in each sequential mailing), to mail to segments of the list based on various separate or overlapping queries, and to collect and store data returned from the emarketing efforts.

With an effective emarketing system you will have the ability to select the mailing sequence based on responses to early mailings and convert prospects who receive one autoresponder series to customers who receive another.

An effective system will keep track of the up sells and cross sells so dear to the marketing world and will allow mailings to be sent to audience members based on the level of interest the members have shown and their buying records to date.

Viral Marketing

What every Internet marketer is looking for, what every magazine publisher wants, is an ultimately powerful viral campaign. There is a world of potential readers and site participants out there, and they all know someone who knows someone who loves your subject matter. How to get to them?

Last year well over 50 percent of magazine publishers intended to make a viral campaign an important part of their Internet marketing strategies. Yet of those publishers who implemented a viral campaign, by far the great majority found it disappointing or ineffective.

Because Internet marketing is still young and benchmarks are still being established and recorded, it's easy to be seduced by anecdotal tales of wondrous campaigns that went around the world six times in twenty four hours and resulted in untold riches for their founders. And it is equally easy to find that once an mailing is released, pass along is small, click-throughs are smaller, and as for conversion, perhaps only a handful of people are added to a list as a result.

Still, it's not impossible to create and execute a successful campaign if it is well conceived, well thought out, and well planned.

As part of the planning stage, think about what is of value to the audience you are trying to reach. Too often, a viral campaign is a simple matter of a "forward to a friend" button on an email, or a suggestion to pass along a bit of news or information. Even outright sell pieces might ask for a pass along in the forlorn hope that, since it's so easy to hit forward, some recipients will surely do so.

However, a "forward to a friend" is far from the basis for an effective viral campaign. A proper viral campaign consists of very specific steps.

It begins with the creation of a product that is of value to your list members and might inspire them to forward it. This could be a very special interactive greeting card, a timely or warm message, or an e-postcard.

It could be a funny or information-packed video. In the Internet world, video is viral. In 2007, 127 million people viewed online video at least once a month. Of those people, a full 76 percent told a friend about what they'd seen.

Viral video, in fact, may be the closest thing we have at the moment to an online version of word of mouth advertising. A video clip, forwarded along with a note from a friend ("hey, I thought you might like to take a look at this, it's hilarious/fascinating/really useful") is one thing that can and does take off in the online world.

What kind of videos get forwarded? Funny ones, of course—isn't that what you get most often, and what you forward the most?—also weird ones; scary ones (remember the bionic burger?); inspirational videos; and useful videos.

They don't have to be complicated. You could do a slideshow with music and subtitles, a humorous staged video, or a remix/montage of clips from other videos (like the ones using candidates clips to make sometimes unexpected statements). They don't have to be long. Two to three minutes is ideal.

With viral video, your conversion element could be as simple as a URL posted on the last slide or the last ten seconds of the video. "For more videos like this, visit . . . " or, "to see the rest of this video, come to our site at. . . [your Web site here]." Whatever it is, do not forget to add some kind of call to action.

Yet another viral offering could be a piece of software or an online application that is fun, interesting, or useful to your market.

Having determined what your viral mailing is to be, here are the two most important separate steps of a viral mailing:

Step one: Begin by emailing to your seed list. Your mailing could be so good that you are convinced that your group will forward it on; but to add some insurance to that, you might make access to your freebie contingent upon your seed group members' putting in a name, or two names, or three names of colleagues, friends, or peers they think would be interested in what you are offering.

In any case, the first mailing will deliver your seed group to a landing page offering the editorial content along with the encouragement or requirement to "pass it on."

Step two: When the friends names are submitted, an email offering the same viral gift is sent from the seed name to the new names, with a "thought you might like this" kind of message. The second generation group is delivered to a landing page offering the same options—the editorial and the option or cost-of-access of referring a friend. At the same time, the second-generation group is invited to opt in to your list.

It's important to remember that these steps are not one and the same. Getting the email address for the referral mailing is not the same as getting an opt-in from the second or subsequent generations of referrals. Those opt-ins must be collected as a separate step of a process that includes converting the new names and at the same time encouraging a continued spread of the original viral product.

Always remember when doing viral mailings that the message can't be commercial. This isn't a sales letter. You don't want hide who you are, but keep your approach content- and connection-based.

The best use of viral marketing is to bring people to your Web site and ideally convert them to a list there. Even if you intend to follow soon afterward with a sales sequence, turn them into friends, fans, and audience members first.

Launch Marketing

Also called "event marketing" by some of its proponents, the concept behind launch marketing is that every sale you make should be offered as an event. Instead of "come to my site any time you want and sign up for my magazine/special report/ebook/webinar/seminar," the idea becomes "on this day at this time we are launching this product. Be there and be part of it."

Even if the product is offered on an ongoing basis, using launch marketing tactics you concentrate your efforts into periodic launch events. The purpose is to build anticipation. The idea is clear: to generate excitement and a sense of timeliness that doesn't exist for a regular product.

Launch marketing at retail stores might involve sales events: back to school, holiday season, one-day-only, red tag, blue light—whatever. On the Internet, the event can be a special sale or a new product or a new iteration of an old product, or an old product that hasn't been offered in a while but now will be, for a limited time only and then never again.

It's all being done, and the art or science behind it is to generate suspense, build desire, tease and tantalize, and then make a big splash. The bigger the splash, the bigger the money made.

The *process* of launch marketing is to build the excitement and get the commitment of your list through the familiar techniques of scarcity (limiting the spaces, assigning deadlines); results in advance (using videos and teleseminars to preview the event); creating a buzz (with copywriting and affiliations); and calling people to action (again, using deadlines to force a decision). A technique often used is inviting your list members to sign up for an early notification—they may be offered, for example, a two-minute head start on the rest of the list.

The most crucial elements of launch marketing techniques are (1) great copywriting and sales techniques, and (2) affiliations:

Copywriting and sales techniques: If you're really going to build excitement for any product, subscription, or series, large or small, if you're going to make an event of your offering, you have to have compelling sales copy. You need to show your audience that this event is exciting, a show, something to engage and delight them.

What some marketers seem to be forgetting these days is just how easy it is for intended recipients to sideline their work. It's now so much easier to mark a sender junk mail or to unsubscribe from a list than it ever was to sort through your mail at the post office and dump it into recycling. So a launch series has to be more, a lot more, than a series of letters talking about how great the product is going to be. It has to use all of the copywriting techniques described in chapter 9, and it has to do it in a way that keeps the mail recipient interested, involved, and looking for the next release.

Affiliations. This has become the backbone of launch marketing. The concept is to shock and awe with a completely united front among all the marketers in your category. Which brings us to the unique online world of affiliate marketing:

Affiliate Marketing

In the old world of magazine publishing, we learned to distrust the concept of partnering with the competition. Sure, you'd do it; you'd join a group like the Music Magazine Publishers Association (MMPA) for example, which gets music titles into specialty accounts, and use the power of the group to market. Sure, you'd work with the category manager or rack quarterbacks to become part of a united program going out to the magazine retailers. But we really didn't go out of our way to create united programs with our competitors, did we?

The world of the Internet is a different place. Internet marketers see the power of affiliations as one of the most powerful tools available to anyone seeking to do business online. And yes, that means partnering with competitors, including direct ones.

Affiliations can include selling the competition's information product on your site, exchanging links, joining each other's groups and fan clubs, and picking up each other's blogs. It means posting your content on other people's sites, and picking up their content for your site.

Mostly it means promoting each other's stuff. Jeff Walker of the "sideways sales letter" says that nothing but affiliate marketing can turn a hundred thousand dollar market into a million dollar market, or a million dollar market into a ten million dollar market; nothing but affiliate marketing can create a groundswell of excitement and support for the new things you're coming out with; nothing but affiliate marketing can create the "united front" that inspires trust and confidence in a site's audience members and brings them along for the exciting times ahead.

Affiliate marketing, Walker tells us, is how we build the market itself. We grow it from a little niche to a happening place through the power of our peers and our mutual support of each other. The mutual support doesn't erode our own market share, according to this thinking. In fact, as we give one another our endorsements, our links, and our outspoken support, it expands the market to the point where there is more for everyone.

And according to the experience documented in the markets in which this thinking is being implemented, the market doesn't tire of the product launches and offerings. Instead, lists become more receptive, more eager to see what the next offering might be.

Sounds weird, doesn't it? But like it or not, Web 2.0 is a reciprocal kind of place: Friend me and I'll friend you; join my group and I'll join yours. As we build unity and trust, we bring the market along in the leaps and bounds of growth we are experiencing.

Or, as StomperNet's Don Crowther puts it, "On the Internet there are no competitors, there are only business partners who don't know it yet."

So following the affiliate marketing model, the next time you have a product to offer, a seminar to launch, or a subscription to promote, go to all the sites in your category. Offer them a big percentage of every sale they bring you—the bigger the percentage, the more enthusiasm they'll show for what you do. Give them everything they need to promote you, give them all the sales letters (that's right, write them for them, a different version for each affiliate) about how great your product is. Call them or mail them and let them know that everyone in your category is part of this program, and you hope that they'll join too. Suggest that they add bonuses of their own for sales made through their mailings and sites, and then give them support too: Let your customers know that bonuses are being offered for those sales by these people.

And then, when they are doing their own sales efforts, support them in return.

Another aspect of affiliate marketing, of course, is to get the commissions from the sales of specific products that result following a visit to your site. When one of your site visitors clicks through to another site and makes a purchase there, a portion of that sale will come to you. In many cases your online advertisers are typically only willing to pay for actual clicks or even actual sales. An affiliate relationship will give you a percentage of that sale.

This aspect of site monetization is currently underutilized by many magazine publishers. It can be very easy to set up—a matter of copying over some code—and it puts you in the path of transactions that you are essentially part of in any case by virtue of links and clicks.

A savvy affiliate marketer will test percentage commission against conversion rate. For example, a link to Amazon might give you only three percent commission on sales versus perhaps ten percent from an independent vendor. The sales on the click to Amazon, however, might be much greater than the conversion on the independent site, due to the trust people have in the Amazon site, so that the volume compensates for the lesser commission amount.

A Final Word

We have progressed, somewhat awkwardly, through the synergies represented by TV, and CD, and DVD, and the earlier stages of putting content up on the Internet. Where we have come to is a world of opportunity so vast that it appears limitless.

Perhaps the next logical step is to create individualized holographic persocoms—part personal computer, part android—to live with each human and meet one's information and entertainment needs; or perhaps we're only a step away from implanting tiny chips in each of our scalps to consolidate our communication, education, entertainment, and social flow of attention.

But for now we have a medium whose powers, whose range, whose flexibility is so great that we in the world of magazine publishing have only begun to reap its fullest benefits. Even so, with all the resources already at our command, we can say again now with confidence, *The Internet is the greatest thing that ever happened to magazine publishers!*

Resources

If resources are a problem remember: You don't have to reinvent the wheel. Individualized programming is fine when you have the luxury of adequate resources. If you don't have that luxury, remember: A blog is a few keystrokes away at WordPress, Movable Type, or any of the many other open source sites wherein the completed software with most of the applications you're looking for resides.

A social networking site can be set up in five or ten minutes at Ning or elsewhere. An entire Web site can be set up after a few minutes with a user manual or tutorial using resources from Yahoo, Google, NetObjectsFusion, or elsewhere.

IT support can be gotten for unthinkably low prices through Elance, Rent A Coder, and other sites that specialize in meeting the needs of individuals and companies for contract personnel.

But magazine publishers create: It's their mission, their impetus, and it's what they do well. Most magazine publishers would rather create something entirely their own than use the wealth of free and low cost resources easily available on the Web.

And that's as it should be. That is how the process of creation continues; it's how new things are developed and discovered, new ground broken. And it's how magazine publishers continue to be unique, individualized.

But speed of implementation is also an asset when working in such a dynamic, quickly changing world as ours. So even if you have a longer term goal and the resources to implement it, you might consider short term and interim solutions as well. The list of resources that follows is meant to help you with your immediate as well as long term needs.

WEB RESOURCES

The following list is a mere tip of the iceberg in terms of the resources out there. Any search of the kind of functionality you are looking for is likely to yield many results for free or low cost resources.

Alexa *[www.alexa.com]*: Find out your traffic ranking.

Amazon Mechanical Turk *[www.mturk.com]*: Find tasks, do them, get paid. Or, put money in your account, offer tasks for people to do, get results.

Ask Database *[www.askdatabase.com]*: A search engine for surveys; find niches in your market

Break *[www.break.com]*: Video sharing site "for guys."

Camtasia Studio *[www.techsmith.com/camtasia]*: Software for screen recording and video presentation.

Comment Kahuna *[www.commentkahuna.com]*: A free software download that helps you find blogs in your subject area that you can comment on; identifies blogs that do not use the "nofollow" tag so you can post your actual link. Includes page rank of blog.

Del.icio.us *[http://del.icio.us]*: A social bookmarks manager.

Digg *[http://digg.com]*: A content- and comment-sharing, social-bookmarking site.

Domain Tools *[www.domaintools.com]*: Tools for domains, including "Whois Lookup" and "Domain Suggestions."

DMOZ *[www.dmoz.org]*: The Open Directory Project.

Ezine.com *[www.ezine.com]*: Ezine-related links.

Facebook *[www.facebook.com]*: Social networking utility.

FeedBurner *[www.feedburner.com]*: Put your RSS feeds up here, promote blogs.

FindNot *[www.findnot.com]*: Gives you an untraceable IP address, so your Internet actions can't be watched; many privacy protection options.

Flickr *[www.flickr.com]*: Photo management and sharing.

Freeblogfinder.com *[http://freeblogfinder.com]*: finds blogs for a particular niche.

Free keyword suggestion tool *[http://freekeywords.wordtracker.com]*: Learn what keywords have highest searches per day and find related long tail keywords.

Google Adsense *[https://www.google.com/adsense]*: put google ads on your site and earn revenue from them.

Google AdWords *[http://adwords.google.com]*: create ads and keywords to be advertised by Google, and pay per click.

Google Blog Search *[http://blogsearch.google.com]*: Has a pinging service.

Google Cache *[www.google.com]*: use Google's cache feature to analyze sites' keyword density.

Google Co-op, or Google Custom Search Engine *[www.google.com/coop]*.

Google Reader *[www.google.com/reader]*: A free Web-based reader for RSS feeds. Checks news sites and blogs for new content and sends updates to your email.

Google Toolbar *[www.google.com/intl/en/options]*: A search box tool with a page rank analyzer.

HelloTxt *[http://hellotxt.com]*: Updates your status on all social networking sites at once.

HubPages *[http://hubpages.com]*: A content-sharing, online-publishing, make-your-own page site.

HTTrack Website Copier *[www.httrackcom]*: downloads an entire site to your computer so you can browse it without being online.

Jaiku *[www.jaiku.com]*: A social-networking, microblogging site.

Jott *[http://jott.com]*: converts voice to text for emails, text messages, etc.

LinkedIn *[www.linkedin.com]*: A social networking site specifically geared toward professionals.

Magazine Dojo *[www.magazinedojo.com]*: a social-networking and support site for magazine professionals.

Marketleap *[www.marketleap.com]*: Search engine services that let you check your link popularity, and see how you compare to your competitors.

Mequoda Group *[www.mequoda.com]*: Internet strategy for publishers, plus marketing advice and Web site design.

Mixiv *[www.mixiv.com]*: Monetize your podcasts.

Mogulus Live Broadcast *[www.mogulus.com]*: Make a channel and broad casts, which you can imbed elsewhere.

Movable Type *[www.movabletype.org]*: Publishing platform and weblog management.

The Music Bakery *[www.musicbakery.com]*: Royalty free music.

MyBlogLog *[www.mybloglog.com]*: shows you who visits what sites.

MySpace *[www.myspace.com]*: Social networking.

NetObjects Fusion *[www.netobjects.com]* Web site design software.

Niche Watch *[www.nichewatch.com]*: Keep track of competitors for specific keywords.

Ning *[www.ning.com]*: An online create-your-own-social-network service.

Oneupweb *[www.oneupweb.com]*: Helps clients gain high positions on search engines.

OptiLink *[www.optilinksoftware.com]*: a tool for evaluating your competitors' backlink reputation.

Orbit Downloader *[www.orbitdownloader.com]*: Download music and video, etc., from YouTube, MySpace, and other sites.

Ping-o-Matic *[http://pingomatic.com]*: Set your blogs to ping to notify search engines, etc., of new content.

Pownce *[http://pownce.com]*: A social networking site with a focus on sending things, such as files, links, etc.

PRWeb Press Release Newswire *[www.prweb.com]*: Online news and press release distribution.

PremiumCast.com *[www.premiumcast.com]*: A package with podcast, RSS, and marketing technologies.

Propeller *[www.propeller.com]*: A social news portal, part of the AOL network.

Pushbuttonvideomarketing *[www.pushbuttonvideomarketing.com]*: Makes and uploads video for you.

Riva Video Experience *[www.rivavx.com]*: Video authoring; lets viewers decide what to see next.

RssReader *[www.rssreader.com]*: Free RSS reader.

Search Engine Text *[www.searchenginetext.com]*: Shows you what text is on any given Web site.

SearchStatus *[www.quirkbiz/searchstatus]*: Using Mozilla or Firefox as a browser, check "Highlight Nofollow Links" and it will highlight them in pink.

SEO Elite *[www.seoelite.com]*: Software to evaluate your competitors' backlink reputation.

SEO Hosting *[www.seohosting.com]*: Web hosting services for search engine optimization.

Site Sniper Pro *[www.sitesniperpro.com]*: Utility for AdWords180.

Squidoo *[www.squidoo.com]*: Free page-building site.

StomperNet *[www.stompernet.com]*: A members-only support site for entrepreneurs.

StumbleUpon *[www.stumbleupon.com]* A Web-browser plugin with which users discover and rate Web pages, videos, etc.; a social bookmarking site.

Submit To iTunes *[www.paulcolligan.com/sumit-to-itunes]*: Submit podcasts to iTunes.

SurveyMonkey *[www.surveymonkey.com]*: Make surveys and analyze the results.

TagCrowd *[http://tagcrowd.com]:* Scans a blog or site and gives a "tag cloud"—visual.

Technorati's "Tags by Popularity" *[http://technoratti.com/tag]*: What tags are popular that hour, that day.

Textalyser *[http://textalyser.net]*: Find out all sorts of things about your text from word count to readability and difficulty; also points out things like repeated phrases.

TubeMogul *[www.tubemogul.com]*: Upload a video here, and it automatically loads to other video sharing sites.

Twitter *[http://twitter.com]*: A free social networking and microblogging service.

Traffic Geyser *[www.trafficgeyser.com]*: Strategy to get high rankings for video on Google.

W3C Markup Validation Service *[http://validator.w3.org]*: Check the markup (HTML, XHTML...) of Web documents.

WordPress *[http://wordpress.org]*: Personal publishing platform and blogging software.

Wordtracker *[www.wordtracker.com]*: see "Free keyword suggestion tool."

Yahoo! *[www.yahoo.com]*: A global Internet services company.

YouTube *[www.youtube.com]*: A video sharing website now owned by Google.

ABOUT THE AUTHOR

Linda Ruth is President & CEO of PTSS (Publishers Total Sales Services)

Ms. Ruth is an internationally known consultant on the keys to audience development at retail and online. She offers advice to communication companies worldwide on how to create effective marketing plans, enabling publishers to maximize their audience development efforts, and launch new publications.

Ms. Ruth is one of the original founders of Women in Periodical Publishing and a current board member.

She is President of Newsstands of America, the coop of independent booksellers. Linda has over 20 years of experience in magazine marketing, and has held management positions at McGraw-Hill and IDG Communications.

Linda Ruth can be found on the Internet at:

Her Social Media site — www.magazinedojo.com
Her Twitter Page — Linda_Ruth.com
Her RSS Feed — www.singlecopysales.com/blog
Her Facebook Pages - Linda Ruth, Independent Publishers Institute, & Magazine Dojo

To email Linda Ruth — lruth@PublishingDojo.com

Made in the USA
Monee, IL
29 December 2020

55647768R10062